Rule # 1

Crazy People
Make You Crazy

At Work Edition

The Survival Guide to Coping with
Impossible People

John Patterson

Jim Duffy - Editor
Mark Hill – Illustrator

Spring Branch Farm – Publishing

Spring Branch Farm, LLC - Publishing
PO Box 186
Butler, Maryland 21023

Rule #1 – Crazy People Make You Crazy – 1st Edition
John J. Patterson
Hard Cover - ISBN 978-0-986194221
Paperback – ISBN 978-0-986194214
Kindle = ISBN 978-0-986194207

Cover design by Janine Sanchez

0615201501

Dedicated to my loving and ever supportive wife - Katharine

Contents

Prologue - The Birth of Rule #1

Everyone encounters crazy, impossible people in their lives.

How do I know this? Well, this is a subject I've been interested in for more than three decades now. My first real job was as a salesman in a stereo store, and the guy who owned that business was flat-out crazy. Later, I moved into computer programming. Then came a stretch as a partner in a big consulting firm, followed by stints as chief operating officer at two different companies.

I encountered crazy people in every step on that journey. As my curiosity about this phenomenon grew, I would often bring the topic up in casual conversation with others. Every time I did, I would hear hair-raising stories from people about the crazy people doing crazy things in their lives.

I don't think I ever heard anyone say, "I don't know what you're talking about."

That was true in all kinds of crowds, whether it was factory hands or executives or schoolteachers or middle managers or full-time moms—you name it.

The conversations all shared a common thread, too, and that also crossed any lines of class and gender and ethnicity that I noticed. Everyone found dealing with impossible people to be the same sort of experience. It was emotionally draining. It left them feeling tired, irritable, and even depressed. Worst of all, it kept them from devoting time and emotional energy to things in life that are much more important.

Crazy people really do make us crazy.

Rule #1 has been a long time in the making. Its origin dates to the early 1990s when I worked at a consulting firm that helped big corporations create and install some powerful new database systems that were just then becoming available.

One day a boss called me and two other mid-level managers in for a chat. He presented us with, as he put it, "the opportunity of a lifetime." It involved moving to Atlanta and leading the team of 50 that would install a complicated new billing system for a utility company.

Some things never change. When a boss in the corporate world talks up the "opportunity of a lifetime" to ambitious young managers, more often than not it all ends up being a euphemism for, "Don't expect to see your spouses and kids for a couple of years."

My workdays in Atlanta generally started with a 6 a.m. managers' meeting and ended around midnight. My wife, Katharine, was caring for our two children, a four-year-old and a one-month-old. Most days, she would be asleep when I left in the morning, and she'd be asleep when I returned home. She laughs today about how the "together" part of our life together in Atlanta consisted of her waking up briefly twice a day to the clatter of a noisy garage door just below our bedroom.

Every systems job has its share of glitches and frustrations, and we ran into an array of such headaches in Atlanta. We managed to work our way through the bulk of them, but a couple of issues proved problematic.

They lingered on, day after day. Every time victory seemed just over the hill on one of these problems, it turned out there was a bigger hill just over the rise. Days stretched into weeks, weeks into months. The job started to resemble a spot-removal operation straight out of Dr. Seuss's *The Cat in the Hat*.

Along the way, the three of us managers began to sense that these intractable problems shared something in common. They weren't programming issues as much as they were *people* problems, in the sense that the people working on them were behaving in irrational, nonsensical ways. It was almost as if they were operating in a parallel universe out of a science fiction film, one where the rules of logic are completely different than the ones here on Earth.

Eventually, the three of us ended up on the brink of despair. Then, during one of those 6 a.m. meetings, my colleague Rick stood up, walked to a whiteboard, and picked out a marker.

"OK, what we're dealing with here are problems that the three of us have never seen before," he began. "We should start at the beginning. Let's at least give these problems names. Right about now, I am thinking that most of the names should be quotes from disaster movies."

We took Rick's joke and ran with it. At every turn from there on in dealing with our intractable problems, we'd invent a wacky name for the trouble at hand. There was "FUD," "The Bag of Shit Theory," and "First Guy on Paper Wins," among others.

A funny thing happened as we built out Rick's whiteboard. The joke slowly evolved first into something half-serious, and then it started to reveal surprising truths about the situation we were in. If you've skimmed the table of contents, you already know that several of the chapter titles in this book are taken straight off of that whiteboard.

Perhaps the most striking thing that we noticed was the way that one of our made-up problem names in particular kept resurfacing at the center of every intractable problem. Not only that, it always seemed to climb to the top of the priority list when it came to solving those problems.

It was called: "Crazy People Make You Crazy."

Crazy people cause crazy problems all by themselves, but the *biggest* danger in what we eventually came to call Rule #1 situations comes not from the crazy person, but from the so-called normal one.

The frustration and confusion that crazy people can cause often leads normal people to behave in abnormal ways. We might start making decisions out of panic or anger. We might lose our temper in the workplace. We might take our troubles home and lash out at spouses and children.

Basically, what we learned in Atlanta is that the second *crazy* in Rule #1 matters even more than the first. No matter how infuriating a situation gets, it's critical to maintain our sanity and our self-control. It was an important first lesson that set me off on a long journey toward developing better ways to recognize and cope with impossible people.

This book is the result of that journey. I hope that it helps you on yours.

INTO EVERY LIFE, A LITTLE RULE #1 MUST FALL.

Rule #1 - Crazy People Make You Crazy

1.0 Who Should Read This Book?

Walk into any big bookstore and the promise of a better life lies just up ahead. In this aisle, the focus is careers. In that aisle, it's relationships. Financial planning is up ahead, with health and spirituality around the bend.

Does the world really need another self-help book? I've been tossing that question around for some time while writing this book, and here, in a nutshell, is why I believe Rule #1 deserves your time:

> *Life is too short and too precious to allow ourselves to be side tracked by impossible people and the impossible problems they create.*

That life is short and precious is a truism, but it's a truism that resonates deeply in the hearts of most everyone I know, especially those of us who've dipped our toes into the waters of middle age or beyond.

Before that, in our 20s and 30s, getting sidetracked here and there by impossible people didn't seem like such a big deal, especially if it involved getting the chance to advance in our career despite a crazy boss or show our creative talents to the world despite an impossible band mate.

A few years down the road, that mindset changes. Perhaps the realization comes when we hit a 40th birthday or a 15th wedding anniversary. Maybe it hits during a high school reunion or while helping a daughter move into her dorm room. It might even arrive with a fright, like landing in the ER with chest pain.

All of a sudden life is flying by.

Such moments turn our priorities upside down—or, more accurately, right side up. We become less interested in conquering the world and winning fortune or fame. We become more frustrated by the detours and roadblocks impossible people can throw in our way.

What we want at this new point more than anything is to pay attention to what matters. We want time for precious things—and by that I mean whatever unique combination of family and friends and hobbies and faith and community brings each of us his or her unique sense of joy and fulfillment.

When all is said and done, that's what this book is about—helping people pay attention to their precious things. The tips and strategies outlined in these pages will empower people to protect their time and their emotional energy from the distractions presented by impossible people.

That's what makes this a genuinely different kind of self-help book.

1.1 The Seesaw

Crazy people are everywhere. They work in hospitals, schools, factories, and office buildings. They live in big cities, suburbs, and small towns alike. They volunteer in church groups, parent teacher associations, neighborhood watch teams, and every other kind of civic organization.

Chances are, there's one in your family. That messy topic is not covered here. Impossible people in family situations often create impossible situations that have unique kinds of issues and complications. Family craziness is a book unto itself—perhaps I will write it someday.

Let's talk here for a moment about that word, *crazy*. When I use it here, I hope it's obvious that I'm not employing it in some clinical sense. We're talking about the everyday brand of crazy in this book. Have you been on the highway, behind some guy going 49 miles an hour and then, once you flip your turn signal and begin to pass him, he speeds up and then speeds up even more—until it ends up you're both going 80 miles an hour?

You end up muttering to yourself, "What is wrong with this *crazy* guy?"

That's the way I'm using *crazy* in this book. It's not meant in the medical sense. No one is suggesting that someone should be committed to an institution.

The sheer number of these non-clinical crazy people in the world didn't truly become clear to me until I began talking up the concept for this book at parties and other social gatherings. I'd toss this book idea out there to see what sort of reaction it elicited.

Every time, the conversation took right off, and other guests jumped right in with horror stories about the impossible people in their lives. It became apparent to me that pretty much everyone has Rule #1 stories to tell, and that means there must be a whole lot of crazy people out there.

The stories I heard ran the gamut of modern life. There were people who thought it a miracle that the whole economy does not collapse as a result of the dumb things that crazy bosses tend to do. Others told tales about crazy customers who come into their businesses expecting to buy every item on the shelves for 50% off the sale price.

Customers had tales of their own to tell, usually about shop owners who aren't just bad at customer service, but who behave day after day in rude and inattentive ways. And I suspect it won't come as a surprise to hear that home-improvement contractors rank among the most common Rule #1 topics of all.

Telling stories like these can be lots of fun. It can even be necessary sometimes, as a way to release some of the stress and tension in a Rule #1 situation. But amid the laughter and the sympathy that such stories generate, I'd like to emphasize here at the outset one key point to make sure things are in the proper perspective.

Everyone has a little Rule #1 inside, and everyone allows a little Rule #1 craziness to show now and again. That includes me, and that includes you.

Think of a seesaw on a playground. You spend some time on the ground and some in the air. Most people spend the vast majority of their seesaw lives in that grounded position. But every one of us has had a few ungrounded moments in life, too. Up there, we are no longer attached to the logic and patterns of day-to-day living. We are no longer abiding by the norms of decent behavior and polite society.

We throw a silly tantrum. We do something hurtful towards a loved one. We act very selfishly on a bad day. Much as we'd like to forget such moments, it's actually important that we remember them when dealing with Rule #1 situations. A little humility goes a long way in coping with impossible people.

Rule #1 people seem to spend most of their seesaw lives drifting up in the air, detached from those basic concepts and rules that grounded people recognize—things like common sense, logical thinking, and the importance of reciprocity and fair play. As a result, they behave in unpredictable ways and tackle tasks with different agendas and priorities than most everyone else.

Rule #1 people also tend to be emotionally adrift, unable to see a situation the way others view it—and especially their own part in it. It's always someone else who should feel guilty, not them. It's always someone else who did them wrong, not the other way around. It's always someone else who needs to apologize.

When Rule #1 situations get emotional—and they often do—people frequently struggle to understand what Rule #1 people are talking about. Their irrational passions can play out at times like devious emotional gamesmanship, but most of the time that's not really what's going on.

Crazy people are more illogical than immoral. Their thought patterns and their emotional makeup simply do not follow any familiar patterns. This tends to make Rule #1 situations difficult for the rest of us to process, let alone respond to.

A big part of the challenge here is simply recognizing in a timely way when Rule #1 is in play. As we'll see in the pages ahead, crazy people often seem perfectly reasonable on first impression. They can come across as congenial, competent, and reliable. It's almost always easy to recognize them in hindsight, but it can be quite hard to see them clearly at the outset.

One reason for this is that people who live life in the grounded seesaw position usually learn by experience to give others the benefit of the doubt. Everyone has met people over the years who seemed a bit off early on. Perhaps they showed an obsessive-compulsive tic or two. Maybe they seemed irrationally thin-skinned about criticism. Or maybe they simply got sidetracked and failed on their first assignment on the job.

In the end, though, most such people turn out to be decent co-workers. Some of them even grow into friends over time. Going forward, those positive outcomes become a part of our social expectations. When we come across behavior that's a little bit strange or unusual, we don't want to jump to conclusions. We don't want to be judgmental. We want to assume the best of a new acquaintance and be sure that the person gets a second and often a third chance before we make any final judgments.

Several of the Rules in this book will be devoted to giving readers a better grasp of the early warning signs that distinguish an everyday false alarm from a genuine Rule #1 problem. Making that distinction as early as possible will help put you in a better position to cope with the coming craziness.

1.2 Why a "Survival Guide"?

The subtitle of this book is "The 10-Rule Survival Guide for Coping with Impossible People." The decision to put those words on the cover was not made casually, but out of a desire to set proper expectations.

This is a book about survival, not world domination.

Plenty of books out there promise great victories over rivals and competitors in the business world. This is not one of those books. I didn't want readers to open up *Rule #1* expecting to learn how to emerge as the *winner* in their *battles* with the impossible people in their lives. This is not *The Art of War*.

The truth is that this book is not so much about crazy people and how to get rid of them. Rather, it's about the way we handle ourselves around impossible people—and, especially, about the way we go about making sure to take care of our responsibilities in Rule #1 situations.

The key to doing that successfully is paying attention to the person in the mirror. It's your own attitude and your own actions that will help to keep Rule #1 people at bay. The tools and strategies in the chapters ahead are designed to help you keep your cool, while steering clear of the emotional drama that tends to follow Rule #1 people around like the cloud of dust that's always trailing Charlie Brown's friend Pigpen.

However, this is not a license to up and walk away from a crazy situation. This is where our responsibilities come in. We need to remember our obligations, whether owed to bosses or patients or students or colleagues. Those obligations matter.

A couple of magazine editors I know showed me one way to look at this when they told me about the approach they took when story drafts from writers arrived in disastrous shape. These drafts were frequently on strong subjects with a lot of potential. Much like the trio of managers in Atlanta that I wrote about in the Prologue, the editors had visions of glory and prizes in mind when they made the story assignments.

Upon seeing a draft in dreadful shape, however, the first thing these editors learned to do was take a deep breath and adjust expectations. They put their visions of glory aside. They focused instead on an achievable goal. The responsibility they had to their readers and to the publisher was to lift those bad drafts up to a level that was worthy of publication—something that was worth a reader's time.

That's the kind of approach I'm talking about in the subtitle to this book. When dealing with Rule #1 people, the first step is to reset our own expectations. Sometimes that will involve revising our goals downward. But it should never mean that we lower expectations to a level where we are no longer meeting our workplace obligations or maintaining our professional standards.

1.3 The Rain in Ireland

My sister went on a vacation to Ireland a few years back. When I asked her how she enjoyed the trip, she jumped straight into gushing with boundless joy.

"Wonderful!" she said. "It was such a beautiful, enchanting place filled with these incredibly warm and happy and generous people. Standing on the Cliffs of Moher, that was just one of the great experiences of my life—something I'll never forget. It was almost mystical." She went on and on about the experience and how she couldn't wait to go back again.

"How was the weather?" I asked when I was able to find a crack in her enthusiasm.

"Oh, it rained *every* day," she said with a laugh, waving that question off like it was nothing.

Take note of this anecdote. It seems such a simple little story, doesn't it? But it captures perfectly the first critical step on the journey towards learning new and better ways to cope with impossible people.

That first step involves, above all else, an attitude adjustment. We need to start regarding crazy people in the way my sister regarded the rain in Ireland—as something so inevitable as to be unremarkable. No one is going to live a life free from rain. No one is going to live a life free from Rule #1 situations.

Into every life a little Rule #1 must fall.

We can choose to moan and cry about impossible people and situations—in the way that so many people do complain about the weather when it takes a bad turn. Or we can strive to be like my sister on her travels and live our lives in the spirit of the old saying, "There is no such thing as bad weather; there is only bad clothing." Set the right expectation and be prepared.

If we prepare ourselves, the rain will not ruin our day. Don a jacket, put on some boots, and pick up an umbrella. Then head out into that rain confident that it is irrelevant to how the day is going to turn out.

It's true that some Rule #1 storms will be worse than others. There are impossible people out there who are crazy on levels that can be hard to fathom until we experience them in person. Some Rule #1 people can be almost like forces of nature, more like hurricanes and tornados than the downpours my sister experienced in Ireland.

But the principle remains the same. The most important preparation we can make for Rule #1 encounters involves our mindset and our emotional reactions. If we accept the inevitability of crazy people in our lives, their appearance will not seem so much of a disruption. If we prepare for them in the way my sister prepared to endure the Irish rain—with the right attitude and coping skills, that is— they will no longer sap our energies and leave us emotionally drained.

People really can learn to deal with Rule #1 situations in ways that help them maintain their sanity and preserve their reputation. They can emerge from Rule #1 situations with an outcome that comes as close as possible to doing right by their company, their co-workers, and their loved ones.

Helping people reach that point is the purpose of this book. Picture a day in the future, one spent dealing hour after hour with a difficult and challenging Rule #1 situation. Now imagine that day ending with an echo of the exchange between my sister and me after she returned from Ireland.

"How was everything at the office?"

In response, we smile and wave all those hours away. "Oh, it was one crazy thing after another."

1.4 A Cautionary Word about "Crazy"

If you have the hardcover version of this book, take a moment right now to remove the book jacket. Take another moment and turn that cover inside out to see what's on the other side.

Yes, it's a fake cover. I like to think of it as the "New York City subway" version of our book jacket. Can you imagine riding the subway and having some wild-eyed, edgy New York character catching a glimpse of the title of this book? *Crazy People Make You Crazy*. The thought puts visions of Robert DeNiro in *Taxi Driver* in my mind.

"You readin' 'bout *me*?"

That's not going to happen if he thinks you're reading *Anthology of Poems* by Woodyard Kindling.

The fake cover is all in good fun, but it also aims to communicate an important point about the use of the word *crazy*. Back in Atlanta, in the early days of Rule #1, we chose that word precisely because it's a little bit out on a limb. That's what makes it catchy, memorable, and fun. Plus, it made us laugh, and laughter is indeed a strong medicine when you're grappling with the kind of stress that Rule #1 situations can bring on.

However, we were also careful to keep the word among ourselves, using it only within our circle of three top managers.

Crazy is still catchy and memorable after all these years, but it's also still a loaded word. We need to keep the use of that word within bounds. That means it stays in these pages and never gets used in public.

There is a belief among certain observant Jews that the name of God should never be spoken aloud. The thinking behind it is that by never using the name, the possibility that it will ever be misused is eliminated.

This is called the Ineffable Name Doctrine. When the word Yahweh appears in print, followers of this doctrine replace it when speaking aloud with either the word *Adonai*, "Lord," or *Ha-Shem*, "The Name."

In this book, we have the Ineffable Insult Doctrine. Basically, we are not allowed to speak the word *crazy* aloud. Ever. We are also not allowed to put it in texts, posts, e-mails, tweets, memos, or any other public communications platform.

The word is never to be used outside of these pages. You should never call a crazy person *crazy*, no matter how crazy things get. Looking a crazy person in the eye and saying, "You're crazy," is always—*always*—a bad idea. It lifts the crazy person up onto the moral high ground and makes him or her a victim of your verbal abuse, at which point the situation just gets worse.

Remember, we all have a little Rule #1 inside. We've all had our moments drifting up on the ungrounded side of the seesaw. We should remain humble here, remembering that at some point in our own lives, somebody out there either already has or someday may have good reason to point a finger in our direction and think, "That person's crazy."

Between the cover, the Prologue and this chapter, the word *crazy* has appeared 56 times so far. Going forward, however, it will start to appear much less often (especially after Rule #2, which is the only other rule with *crazy* in its name). Now that you know what Rule #1 is all about, you'll start reading more often about "Rule #1 people" and "Rule #1 situations." *Crazy* will still pop up now and again, but not nearly as often.

1.5 The Rest of the Rules

Now that you've got the Rule #1 concept down, it's time to get about the business of learning to better recognize and deal with the impossible people in your life.

The chapters that follow are organized in straightforward fashion. Chapters 2, 3, and 4 focus on the warning signs that will help you recognize more quickly when Rule #1 is in play. Here, you'll learn what the Abbott and Costello routine "Who's On First" has to do with all of this. You'll also get an introduction to the concept of "FUD." And you'll learn when it's time to "Count the Bricks."

Chapters 5 through 10 are devoted to strategies and tools that will bolster the odds that you'll emerge from a Rule #1 situation with an acceptable outcome. The rules outlined in these chapters range from the cautionary—"If It Feels Good, Don't Say It"—to the empowering—"First Guy on Paper Wins." Here, too, is the invaluable "Bag of

Shit Theory." You'll also learn how to try your luck at a "Freudian Coin Toss."

The Rules are structured in a common format. The Concept will introduce the topic. A series of examples, stories and observations will be used to enhance the understanding of the Rule. The Bottom Line of each chapter will emphasize the key takeaways of the Rule. Tangents will be extra narratives on related and interesting aspects of the Rules.

Finally, there is "What Have You Learned, Dorothy?" That is the title of Chapter 11, which reviews the key lessons from the book and discusses some of its implications for the way we make the big decisions in our lives, the ones that shape our careers and family lives as well as our dealings with Rule #1 people.

One last reminder, because I can't stress it enough: Remember, going forward in these pages, that this is a survival guide, not a battle plan. Dealing with Rule #1 people is not a matter of achieving victory. It's a matter of managing your emotions and expectations, then making smart decisions that help to protect your time and your reputation while you live up to your responsibilities and obligations.

1.6 The Bottom Line

Remember: Into every life a little Rule #1 rain must fall. Every one of us is bound to encounter some Rule #1 people in life, so don't expect otherwise. And every one of those encounters will present risks of being dragged down into a Rule #1 world that eats up our time and saps our emotional energy.

This book aims to help people better cope with Rule #1 people. This goal is not a matter of triumph or failure. There are no wins and losses here. Rather, our aim is two-fold. First, we want to recognize Rule #1 situations more quickly, before they get out of hand and drag us down. Second, we want to react to Rule #1 situations in ways that are calm, thoughtful, and effective. Keeping our cool is critical. We want to stay on the grounded side of life's seesaw, keeping our emotional selves at a safe distance from the Rule #1 rain.

Rule #2 - Am I Crazy?

2.0 The Concept

Rule #1 situations can be quite disorienting for people who are accustomed to living on the grounded side of life's seesaw. Impossible people have a way of taking day-to-day reality and transforming it into a funhouse mirror. This chapter is devoted to one of the key warning signs that will help you recognize early on when Rule #1 is in play.

Crazy people make for crazy situations. They just do—it's a definitional thing. They will not remember saying things that you know they said. They will not remember hearing things that you know they heard. They will remember saying things that you know they never said, and they will remember hearing things that you know they never heard.

It will make your head spin. It will leave you speechless. It will have you dropping your head into your hands in frustration. Finally, it will leave you asking, "Am *I* crazy?"

Stop right there: That moment of utter confusion is actually a sign pointing the way to clarity. When you ask "Am *I* crazy?" there almost certainly is a Rule #1 person in the room.

But it's not you. It's time to look around and identify the real culprit.

2.1 Who's Crazy on First?

"Who's on first?"

"Yes."

"I mean the fellow's name."

"Who."

"The guy on first."

"Who."

"The first baseman."

"Who."

"The guy playing …"

"Who is on first!"

"I'm asking *you* who's on first!"

In the most famous comedy sketch of all, poor Lou Costello sure seems to be playing the fool. A 5-foot, 5-inch bowling ball of a man, he wears his baseball hat in cockeyed fashion. When he swings a bat, he somehow manages to thwack himself on the back of the head. His tie dangles nearly to his knees, and his voice is that of a whiny child.

Straight man Bud Abbott, by contrast, makes a solid first impression. He wears an impeccably tailored suit. He speaks in calm, cool, and collected fashion. He seems the very picture of a rational man.

Costello: "All I'm trying to find out is what's the guy's name on first base."

"No. What is on second base."

"I'm not asking you who's on second."

"Who's on first."

"One base at a time!"

"Well, don't change the players around."

"I'm not changing nobody!"

"Take it easy, buddy."

As the sketch progressed through outfielders named Why and pitchers named Tomorrow, Costello becomes more and more unhinged. He slaps himself in the head. He buries his face in his hands.

The words "Am *I* crazy?" are not in the script, but they would fit perfectly. Much of the humor in "Who's on First" comes from the fact that Costello's confusion is perfectly understandable. He is being led towards a state of confusion and frustration by an obstinate straight man so divorced from reality that he is unable to recognize the rather obvious source of Costello's confusion.

Poor Costello missed the key warning sign. Rule #2 should have been a wake-up call for him. It should have told him that it was time to snap out of his frustrated state and look at the situation anew, with fresh eyes and calm nerves.

2.2 Rule #1 People Are Good at First Impressions

Here is a crazy thing about Rule #1 people: generally speaking, they don't look or act all that strange as you're first getting to know them. They can seem quite normal. They can even come off as talented and charming.

Often, there is nothing about meeting a Rule #1 person that makes it clear that you are, in fact, meeting a Rule #1 person. It's going to seem like a routine encounter. Afterwards, these are the kind of impressions that you will share with spouses and co-workers.

• "They called me in today and introduced me to the new head nurse on the unit. I'm really hopeful she can make some needed changes."

• "Had a sit-down this morning with the woman in charge of fixing the XYZ project. No worries—I think she should have it sorted out in short order."

• "Our new choir director seems to have it all together. Maybe now that she's on board, singing at church will be fun again."

A part of this phenomenon is simple projection. People living on the grounded side of life's seesaw don't go through life worried that everyone they meet will turn out to be a Rule #1 character. They tend to give new acquaintances the benefit of the doubt.

That is exactly what I did back in Atlanta when I first met Henry, a Rule #1 character who caused us a lot trouble back in my consulting days. If you'll recall from the Prologue, we were working to develop and install a groundbreaking new billing system for a big utility company.

Every systems job has its share of glitches and frustrations, and in Atlanta we worked our way through the usual array of those headaches. But one issue proved especially problematic, and this particular problem was right at the core billing calculation that served as the operational heart of the system.

One thing that made this project so challenging is that we were trying to create a brand new type of billing system. Previously, utilities built completely separate systems for each of their residential, commercial, and industrial divisions. In Atlanta, we were aiming to put all three on a single data flow headed towards a central module where final sorting and calculation would take place. This calculation module is what kept failing in Atlanta.

Henry was the guy in charge of that module. We called him into a meeting. What a relief that session was! Henry seemed to possess the technical skills needed for this challenge. He was well connected inside the company, which is always a plus. Top executives seemed to trust him with critical assignments. Best of all, he seemed earnest, hardworking, and rational.

Henry assured us that the sorting-switch problem wasn't nearly as dire as it looked. We listened to his plans for fixing it. We made a few suggestions. He seemed to take them to heart. I left the meeting breathing a sigh of relief, confident that the problem would be fixed in short order.

I checked in with Henry a few days after that meeting. He told me he was nearly at the finish line. Only a few technical problems remained. The next morning at a meeting, he went so far as to pronounce the whole problem fixed. The news elicited an excited round of backslapping and congratulations.

But that afternoon, Henry ran some additional tests and found another bump in the road. He estimated that he'd need another week to get the calculation running smoothly once and for all. So it went. Victory was just over the hill. But beyond that hill, it turned out there was an even bigger hill. Days stretched into weeks, weeks into months.

We reached a point where the entire Atlanta job—there were more than 100 people involved, each eager to move ahead with their own piece of the job—was basically at a standstill. We were all waiting for Henry. It was starting to feel like *Waiting for Godot*.

2.3 You Can't Make Sense out of Nonsense

Looking back now, it's obvious to me that Henry was Rule #1 through and through. But in the moment, it wasn't so clear at all. I was surprised when Henry failed to make quick progress on the sorting-switch calculation.

Every time he told us he was on the verge of making a breakthrough, some new issue would crop up. And each new roadblock would bring its own fresh array of devilish complications. Every step Henry took to make that calculation work landed us in deeper trouble.

As time went on and we got to know Henry a little bit better, we noticed a couple of idiosyncrasies. He liked to work late into the night, past midnight sometimes. Something about being alone in that giant office building with his thoughts and his plans seemed to appeal to him.

Come morning, he'd arrive a tick later than everyone else. He'd have a slightly haggard look about him, with a five o'clock shadow showing and wearing a shirt that needed ironing. His appearance fairly shouted out how hard he'd worked the night before and how late he'd been toiling away. Was he trying to play the hero?

But everyone has his or her share of idiosyncrasies, right? I still didn't see any reason to worry about Henry. At this point, my management team began devoting even more attention to Henry and the sorting-switch problem. In fact, I had a run of one-on-ones with him, in which the two of us would outline a plan of action for the coming days.

But when I would circle back a few days later to check in with Henry, I'd find him working off plan. He would be off chasing some brand new complication that he'd just discovered. The first couple of times this happened, I gently reminded him that we had an agreed on a plan of action and that he wasn't following it.

He looked me square in the eye and said something completely untrue.

"What are you talking about?" he asked. "We agreed to no such thing."

Come the third or fourth time around with this sort of exchange, I found myself in what I now recognize as Rule #2 territory.

"Am *I* crazy?"

I asked that question quite seriously. I started worrying about all the stress I was under. Was my memory failing? Was I mixing up the content of different meetings with different people? Did I need to take a break and get away for a weekend—*something*?

Those of us who live most of our lives on the grounded side of life's seesaw grow accustomed to operating in a world of logic, reason, and social reciprocity. When everything stops making sense, it's a natural tendency to look in the mirror and wonder what we ourselves are doing wrong.

If I had known then what I know now, I would have stopped worrying about my sanity the moment I found myself thinking, "Am *I* crazy?" I would have realized much earlier on that it was time to start preparing myself for some Rule #1 rain.

Alarm bells should have begun ringing out in my head about Henry. This was a moment when I needed to push anger and frustration aside. I needed to take a deep breath and re-assert control over my emotions.

I would have started to behave like someone who realizes that life is too short for this Rule #1 nonsense—someone who wants to keep the tumult and drama to a minimum while doing as right as possible by co-workers and company.

2.4 Why Are There So Many Rule #1 People?

I haven't worked in the consulting field for quite a few years now, but I still have a bit of the consultant in me. People in that field are famous in the business world for responding to any question that comes along by breaking out a piece of paper and drawing a four-quadrant graph to explain everything that needs explaining.

This sketch on the next page is called the "Can They/Will They" matrix. It's generally employed in the business world to look at individual tasks up close and decide whether and where to deliver training and other assistance.

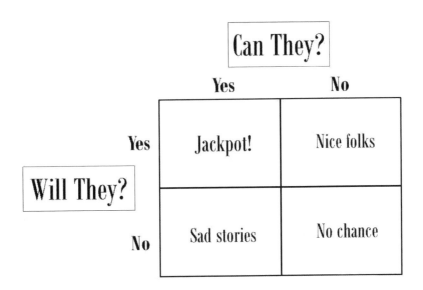

The vertical axis here focuses on the emotions and motivation of workers. Are they willing to do what it takes to get the job done, or not? The horizontal axis looks at their functional abilities. Are they able to do the job? Do they have the skills?

Walking through the four corners we can see that the top left is our happy place. There, we hit the "Jackpot" every time, finding workers who are both motivated and skilled. As long as managers get to work with only people in this corner, everything will turn out just fine.

Problems start to emerge as we move into the top right quadrant. I labeled this square "Nice Folks," because the people here genuinely mean well and are striving for a good outcome. But unlike the willing-and-able jackpot crowd, these folks are willing and *un*able.

Positive outcomes are still possible in the upper-right quadrant. But they will come only after long and potentially painful and expensive delays as managers deliver the combination of training, assistance, and handholding these workers need. Even then, there are no guarantees of a good result.

At lower left are the "Sad Stories." These workers have the skills to do what needs doing but lack the will. They might be lazy, angry, confused—or some combination of the three. Whatever the case, they put these emotional needs first, refusing to set them aside and deal with the tasks at hand in a responsible way.

In the last quadrant, there is simply "No Chance." Here in the darkest corner of the "Can They/Will They" universe, workers have neither the skills nor the motivation to do the job.

The "Can They/Will They" paints a rather bleak picture. In two squares, there is guaranteed failure. In one square, there is, at best, a small chance of success.

The "Jackpot" square is the only corner where things actually get done. But how many managers—with the exception of Miller Huggins, the skipper of the 1927 Yankees—have access to a team that resides one and all in this happy corner of skilled and willing?

Optimistically, the population of workers and relatives won't be distributed evenly between the four quadrants. A 75% chance of wrong person in wrong job would just make us all jump out the window. But if just 10% of the people are in each of the three trouble quadrants, that is 30% bad news all the time.

No wonder it feels like there are so many impossible Rule #1 people out there. The odds are in favor of finding the wrong person in the wrong job.

2.5 The Fight You Cannot Win

There are lots of people out in the world who present difficult challenges but who are not Rule #1 characters. There are short-tempered supervisors, inattentive co-workers, bad teachers, dumb co-workers, and on and on. On our journey through life, we learn quite a bit about how to respond to such people.

Sometimes we need to nurture and encourage such people. Sometimes we need to deliver a dose of tough love. Other strategies land somewhere in between those two, and the toolboxes we turn to in dealing with difficult people tend to be pretty extensive—and pretty effective.

Turning to that rational-world toolbox will be our first instinct when Rule #1 comes into play. We'll want to sit down in a nurturing way and talk things through. We'll want to see if the challenging person in this case needs some extra help or training. We might want to tell them in no uncertain terms that it's time to shape up.

The problem is, every tool in our rational box is useless with Rule #1 people. This is definitional: An impossible, irrational person makes for an impossible, irrational situation. What good are rational tools in these circumstances?

Often, impossible people will not even recognize the things you regard as basic rules of human interaction. There will be no genuine notion in their brains of limits imposed by a sense of politeness or fairness or loyalty or friendship.

Do unto others? Rule #1 people can't grasp the concept.

"Am I crazy?" Rule #1 people never, ever ask that question of themselves.

In the Rule #1 world, scheduling a simple sit-down to discuss problems can be like picking a fight. More often than not, it's a fight you are going to lose.

People like Henry will simply ignore any course of action both of you agree to. They continue to go off on illogical tangents. And when you try to talk with them about why the same mistakes are happening all over again, you will hear things like this:

• "No, we didn't agree to that. I mean, I guess we talked about it, but we never really said it was a final decision."

• "You never told me to do it that way. What are you talking about? Why are you trying to make me look bad?"

• "Yes, of course I remember, but that was before this new and much bigger problem arose. Now everything is different. You're smart enough to see that, aren't you?"

As the situation veers off in such directions—or along some even crazier tangent—it's important to recognize what's happening and to avoid wasting too much time looking in the mirror and wondering if you've lost your mind. The sooner you break out your Rule #1 coping skills, the sooner you'll be able to find refuge from the Rule #1 rain.

2.6 The Bottom Line

The first key sign that you are in a Rule #1 situation comes when you find yourself questioning your own sanity. You will be 100% sure of a memory, only to hear from someone else that it never happened. You will be 100% sure that you never said something, only to hear another insist that you did.

You will begin to wonder if you are crazy. You will start to wonder what is wrong—too much stress, not enough sleep, a failure to focus?

The most likely answer is none of the above. When you start to question your own sanity, there probably is a Rule #1 person in the room, but it's not you. Shake off your confusion and look around for the real source of craziness.

Tangent—The Rank and File Phenomenon

As time went on in the Atlanta job, I noticed another idiosyncrasy about our Rule #1 friend Henry. He didn't seem to have much of a relationship with the rank-and-file workers who toiled on jobs all around his station.

These folks didn't say much of anything to us about Henry. Even when asked directly, they would simply mouth a meaningless platitude or two, nothing more. Nor did they seem at all interested in hopping aboard with his project, despite the fact that it was an important piece of a multimillion-dollar endeavor.

And yet at the same time Henry's bosses spoke glowingly of his work and his dedication.

Over the years, I've come to understand that this is a common dynamic in Rule #1 situations. Rank-and-file workers tend to see through a Rule #1 personality pretty quickly. As the ones on the receiving end of his orders and project plans, they start to develop an intuitive grasp of the faulty logic behind them.

Rule #1 people fool management all the time, but they have a much harder time deceiving co-workers who are actually on the ground with them for any length of time.

One thing that's especially interesting about the Rank-and-File Phenomenon is how these co-workers and underlings behave in a situation like the one in Atlanta. In my experience, they keep their heads down and their noses in their own business.

What they've learned over the years is to stay as far away as possible from the Rule #1 rain. They, too, have learned to steer clear of the drama. It's better to wait out the Rule #1 character—he or she will most likely get promoted or transferred away soon enough.

Rule #3 - FUD: Fear, Uncertainty and Doubt

3.0 The Concept

The theory of this book is that Rule #1 people are not really conscious of what they are doing and how it affects other people. They are simply living in the moment and reacting on instinct to whatever stimuli are in front of them. The craziness they cause is generally not the result of calculation or deviousness.

That makes the next warning sign very interesting. Rule #1 people generally like to keep their craziness under wraps. If they sense that they are about to be uncovered, they often turn in the desperation of the moment to a tactic that amounts to saying, "Look at that other problem over there!"

This phenomenon operates a lot like the human body's instinctive "Fight-or-Flight" response. I've seen it unfold so many times over the years that I think the psychologists should think about changing the name of that instinct to "Fight or Flight or Misdirection."

This chapter will help you recognize those misdirection plays. That, in turn, will enable you to stay focused on the real issues where you can make a difference.

3.1 The Fixer Calls "FUD"

My consulting firm had a specialist they would call in when projects got completely out of hand and ended up in RMS *Titanic* territory. We called this guy The Fixer, and everybody I worked with was in awe of him. He was the best project manager I've ever seen.

The Fixer was old school all the way. There was no charisma in the way he acted and no glamour in the way he dressed. His suits came off the rack. His hair usually looked like it needed combing.

Nor was The Fixer interested in social graces. He didn't do small talk and joshing around. He never delivered pats on the back or uttered sensitive words of encouragement. He was not a water-cooler guy.

He expected you to do your job, and that's basically the only thing he had any intention of talking with you about. How is the job going? Is it done yet? If not, will it be done on time? If not, why not, and how can we fix that problem?

The first time I worked with him, The Fixer knocked me off balance right at the outset. He started throwing around this strange word that I'd never heard before. It sounded like something from another language—German, maybe, or Klingon.

"FUD."

He didn't bother to explain it. And I didn't want to look stupid in front of a company legend, so I didn't ask what it meant.

The word would surface often in the staff meetings he chaired, especially when The Fixer was listening to status reports on one task or another. Those reports often included little detours that began with phrases like, "But what worries me …" or "The risk going forward …" or "The scary wild card here …."

The Fixer had no patience with such detours. "Forget about it," he'd say. "That's all FUD. We don't care about FUD right now."

Over time, I caught on to The Fixer's meaning. The word he was using isn't a word at all, actually—it's an acronym. "FUD" stands for fear, uncertainty, and doubt.

FUD doesn't encompass all varieties of fear and doubt. The term applies specifically to fear and doubt that has been created in order to distract or discourage people who are about to take a certain action or reach a certain conclusion.

In Rule #1 situations, the FUD-makers are often trying to cover tracks that might otherwise reveal their irrational behavior. The projects that The Fixer took over were all failing badly, and that means they were invariably full of FUD. A big part of what made The Fixer such a great manager was his talent for recognizing FUD and pushing it to the side so that he could stay on the path towards turning the project around.

3.2 Rule #1 People Are Full of FUD

Argumentum ad metum. The "Appeal to Fear."

Perhaps you, too, remember this phrase from your college days. That's where I first heard it, while studying elementary logic. *Argumentum ad metum* falls into a category of fallacies known as the "appeals to emotion."

This particular fallacy is often the strategy of choice for Rule #1 people. They tend to be masters of FUD, always dropping little "What about this?" and "What about that?" bombs into the lives of their co-workers and supervisors.

In my experience, Rule #1 people employ this technique when they are coming under a higher level of scrutiny, one that risks revealing some incompetence or illogical behavior on their part. In order to steer that scrutiny away from their corner of the project, they manufacture a potential crisis in some other corner.

Rule #1 people can use FUD in quite intricate ways. This was certainly true of our old friend Henry at the utility company in Atlanta. If you'll recall, he was the guy in charge of fixing a problem with the most critical switching station in a complex new billing system.

The fact that Henry ended up at that all-important switch probably did not happen by accident. Henry was the type of Rule #1 character who loved to play the hero. His type goes to great lengths to maneuver themselves into critical posts where they can feed their need to occupy the starring role in the drama of the workplace.

Once ensconced in such a role, they will zealously guard the secrets of the position, making sure that no one else understands the inner workings of their domain. At that point, people like Henry are in position to "find" critical problems whose solutions will come only through their own heroic efforts.

Every time Henry seemed ready to announce that the critical switch was fixed, he discovered some new crisis that he needed to address or some new glitch that he needed to iron out. What I learned about Henry over time was that deep down he didn't want to fix the switch. If it ever got fixed, everyone would move on from that issue and leave him to suffer through a stretch of anonymity away from the spotlight.

His goal was to make sure that didn't happen. While everyone else was working to tackle the job at hand,

47

Henry was working on keeping himself at the center of a crisis, with all eyes turning to him and counting on him to save the day.

That's why he kept piling on the FUD, in the form of unexpected and mind-boggling new problems at every turn. If I'd have had a better grasp of Rule #3 in my days as young manager, I might have recognized that truth about Henry weeks earlier than I did.

3.3 History of FUD

At first I thought FUD was something The Fixer had invented. I was wrong. The acronym actually has a rich history in the business world that stretches back half a century, to the 1960s.

It was invented by computer pioneer Gene Amdahl, who earned his measure of fame while serving as a key player in the development of some very important products in the evolution of mainframe computing—the IBM 704, the IBM 709, and the System/360.

In 1970 he left IBM and launched the Amdahl Corporation, competing directly with his old employer. He got off to a good start. The Amdahl 470V/6 was less expensive, more reliable, and faster than the IBM alternatives. But it never really took off in the marketplace, a fact Amdahl blamed on FUD-style marketing by IBM salespeople.

Historian Eric S. Raymond summarized the charge: "The idea, of course, was to persuade buyers to go with safe IBM gear rather than with competitors' equipment. This … was traditionally accomplished by promising that Good Things would happen to people who stuck with IBM, but Dark Shadows loomed over the future of competitors."

IBM had it all over Amdahl when it came to longevity, name recognition, and reputation for excellence. Bosses would always understand buying from IBM. Would they understand buying from an upstart firm that they'd never heard of?

IBM salesmen had a line they liked to pull on potential clients if they felt they might be losing a sale to Amdahl: "Listen, no one ever got fired for buying an IBM system."

A couple of decades later, another upstart computer company met a similar fate. A British company that began life as AMS Trading (and eventually became known as AMSTRAD) created the PCW, a machine that when it came to basic word processing was quite a viable computing option available at a rock-bottom price.

These machines had an innovative design and did not need an internal fan to keep things cool. The fan's absence was no danger to data or functionality, but competitors jumped on the issue nonetheless. It was a FUD operation, through and through.

"Whatever you do, don't buy the PCW, unless you want all of your data to melt," salesmen would say, with deep concern etched on their faces, "I know it sounds unbelievable, but the company that made it didn't even bother to put a cooling fan in there!"

PCW salesmen tried and tried to explain how their machines worked, but the FUD won out. At one point, the company behind the PCW actually began installing completely unnecessary fans just so that customers could hear that reassuring hum now and again.

I haven't seen any indication that the computer business has more people with Rule #1 tendencies than other industries, but I was struck while doing research on FUD at just how much of it goes on in the field. Microsoft, for instance, has been a master of the technique.

In the 1990s, the software giant had its eye on a potentially dangerous competitor, Digital Research. DR had just launched their DR DOS operating system, which cost less than Microsoft's MS-DOS5. It also offered more features; it allowed you to run Microsoft software seamlessly; and it racked up rave reviews in the trade press.

In response, Microsoft played two simultaneous games of FUD. The first was to leak a false rumor that they were on the verge of releasing MS DOS6, a system that would crush DS-DOS by offering a slew of new and improved features.

The second bit of FUD was especially inspired. It's known as the "AARD code incident" in computer circles. Basically, Microsoft arranged their software so that if anyone ran it on DR DOS, they would get a popup with the following message:

"Non-Fatal error detected: error #2726
Please contact Windows 3.1 beta support
Press ENTER to exit or C to continue"

If users pressed "C", they went back into DR DOS and everything continued to work just fine. The message was a false alarm, baked into the software by some FUD-savvy technicians. Microsoft ended up in court over that trick. The company eventually settled for a sum rumored to be $280 million.

3.4 Recognizing FUD in the Workplace

Perhaps by this point you've gathered why FUD is so popular with Rule #1 people. Done well, it succeeds. In the workplace, FUD has a way of making you look back at your own plans and do a double take. It brings a distant, unlikely disaster out from the shadows and puts it right before your eyes.

You've studied the specs on that new computer system. You've heard rave reviews from other companies who bought it. You've kicked the tires on this purchase as thoroughly as possible.

And then it comes, the "Dark Shadow": *No one ever got fired for buying an IBM system.*

In thinking about FUD in the workplace, I always go back to my times with The Fixer. Looking back, here are the types of workplace reports that he would just dismiss out of hand as FUD.

• "What if IBM stops supporting this software? I heard a rumor at the conference last week that they might. What happens to us then? Should we have a backup?"

• "The risk here is we get this whole system up and running and then the government regulators show up and refuse to sign off on it. That's why I think we should take steps A, B, and C right now, so we don't end up with egg on our face."

• "What worries me out in the marketplace is Acme Computers. What have they got up their sleeve? They've beaten us to the punch before, you know. If we want to be smart here, we'll start worrying about that."

In the context of The Fixer's projects, questions like these were not ridiculous. But The Fixer had an uncanny ability to separate out all the worries that didn't belong on the table at a given moment from those that really did require immediate attention. He had a gift for staying focused on the things that really matter.

3.5 Fun with FUD in Politics

Politics is another center of FUD expertise. Here are five examples of presidential campaign FUD from recent decades.

• "Daisy," 1964. This infamous campaign ad for Lyndon Johnson opened with a little girl in a field of flowers and closed with a nuclear explosion. In between came some talk about how Johnson's opponent might not be so hot when it came to foreign policy.

• "The Bear," 1980. A bear wanders the woods, to a soundtrack that might have been lifted from "Jaws." Some people don't think the bear is dangerous. Others are committed to being ready, just in case. That latter group includes ardent Cold Warrior Ronald Reagan.

• "Willie Horton," 1988. In Massachusetts, a convicted murderer out on a weekend pass committed kidnapping, rape, and murder. This ad makes is sound like that was exactly the result Gov. Michael Dukakis was hoping for—and exactly the sort of policy he'd be likely to implement if elected president.

• "The Threat," 1998. Bob Dole's supporters dropped a little snippet of "Daisy," then proposed that the little girl from that ad is now all grown up and facing a terrible new threat—drug abuse. Using scenery out of a cheesy black-and-white movie, the ad charged that Bill Clinton would do nothing about this new scourge.

• "The 3am Phone Call," 2008. Once Hillary Clinton started losing ground to newcomer Barack Obama in the battle for the Democratic nomination, she broke out this bit of FUD in which sweet images of "your children" cuddled in bed sound asleep appear against the soundtrack of an emergency phone line ringing in the far-away White House.

3.6 The Bottom Line

One challenging aspect of Rule #1 situations is that they can resemble something of a funhouse mirror. It's hard to keep focused on the core problems at hand when so many crazy things are moving in such unpredictable fashion all around us.

Rule #1 people thrive in such environments. It's not really a devious plot on their part, creating these distractions. Rather, it's a natural outgrowth of their illogical thinking and misplaced motivations. Those of us living on the grounded side of life's seesaw come into a situation with certain expectations of human behavior, and most times those expectations are right on the money.

Rule #1 situations are different. One warning sign that Rule #1 is in play is the presence of these distractions and misdirections that fall into the category of FUD—fear, uncertainty, and doubt. Learn to recognize FUD, and you'll learn to keep your focus on the things that really matter.

Tangent—The Spectrum of FUD Emotions

The most common type of FUD is the "appeal to fear," but it's not the only one. Rule #1 people can also play on other emotions in their efforts to distract people from seeing the true nature of the problem at hand.

Be aware of:

• The Appeal to Pity.
Rule #1 people can be quite adept at playing the pity card. If they need to, they will bemoan the destruction of their career, the ruination of their reputation, and all manner of other imminent woes in an effort to survive the moment and live to fight another day.

Example: "You can't go to the vice president of operations with this problem. It'll ruin my reputation with the company. I'll never get the promotion I've been working for if you do that to me."

• The Appeal to Flattery.
Here, too, Rule #1 people can find the way to generate a distraction from the subject at hand. The praise they deliver can make it more emotionally difficult for managers or co-workers to do what they need to do.

Example: "Yes, there are risks involved, but that's what I recommend we do next. I've got a lot more experience than you in this area, but I know you're smart enough to see that it's the best way to go."

• The Appeal to Spite

Rule #1 people won't feel any qualms about dragging irrelevant personal issues into a situation when they feel it necessary. In an appeal to spite fallacy, someone looks to bring feelings of interpersonal bitterness into an argument where they don't really belong.

Example: "That strategy John Johnson is proposing, well … I'll just say that he's had it in for me for a long time now. I'm sure he's the one who reported me to personnel a couple of years back. It turned out those accusations were completely unfounded."

Rule #4 - Count the Bricks

4.0 The Concept

Rule #1 people are not thinking straight. They are not operating by the standard rules of logic. They don't share the same goals as everyone else on a workplace project. This is why they can often deliver progress reports that are sunny and encouraging when in fact they are making little or no progress.

Here, we focus on the importance of seeking clear, physical, and objective measures of progress when you suspect that Rule #1 is in play. How many pieces of the job are there? How many are done? How many are undone? Unfortunately, the results of such a count in most Rule #1 situations will show that there is a much longer ways to go on the project than everyone thought.

4.1 The Bricklayer

Most people have had Rule #1 adventures with a home-improvement contractor at some point in their lives, so the story of the bricklayer will probably strike a familiar chord. It goes like this:

A woman lives in one city and owns property in another. When she needs some work done on that second property, she uses the Internet and the phone to hire a guy to install a new brick wall as part of a landscaping project.

A week into the project, she gives the bricklayer a call to ask how it's going.

He says, "Almost done—I'm 90% of the way there."

At the end of week two she dials his number again.

And he says, "We're getting very close now—I'd say we're 90% of the way there."

When this same exchange happens at the end of week three, the woman starts to get that "Groundhog Day" feeling.

It's moments like these in life that helped make me a believer in "The 90/50 Theory." Because Rule #1 people are often obsessively focused on winning approval and acceptance in the present moment, they often deliver progress reports that end up being wildly inaccurate.

Your ears should perk up when you hear someone claim that they're "nearly" or "just about" or "90 percent" done. In my experience, I'd say you will be lucky in such cases if the project is 50 percent done. There is actually a pretty good chance that it will in fact be only 5 percent done.

So when you hear someone saying they are 90 percent done, it might be time to start counting the bricks. That's certainly what our property owner should do with her bricklayer.

In this case, the woman can "Count the Bricks" quite literally. How many bricks will there be in a finished wall? How many are up now? What percentage of the way are we towards the finish line? She can then use that information to set the standard for measuring progress going forward in a way that is so crystal clear it might even resonate with a rationality-challenged Rule #1 contractor.

There's an old saying in the business world: "You get what you *in*spect, not what you *ex*pect." That aphorism is especially apt when in Rule #1 situations.

4.2 The Bagel Slicer

One of my more interesting experiences as a young manager involved a woman I'll call The Bagel Slicer. She was new to our team in Atlanta. Like so many Rule #1 people, she seemed at first like a hard worker. She was quite bright, and she had solid technical skills.

I decided to put a little extra on her plate to see how she would respond. The report I asked her to prepare involved a lot of tedious, time-consuming calculations. The project had a hard deadline because I needed to present our findings to a client at an upcoming meeting.

I checked in with The Bagel Slicer regularly. She assured me over and over that she was almost done. "I'm 90 percent of the way there," she'd say. "Just a few odds and ends left."

One Friday afternoon I reminded The Bagel Slicer that I'd need the report on Monday morning, before the client meeting. When Monday morning arrived, she called in sick.

"Well, okay," I said, "but I need that report for the client meeting, so tell me where it is."

"I've got it here at home," The Bagel Slicer said. "But I've got to go to the doctor right now. Call me later and we'll figure it out."

An hour and a half later, she told me that she had the report but that her doctor had warned her that she was very contagious and so she couldn't possibly get the report to me today.

I was having none of it. "I need it this afternoon. Where do you live? I'll come over and get it."

She gave me an address and an apartment number. I went there and knocked on the door. No one answered. By this point, Rule #2 was definitely in play, as I was standing outside that door with my head in my hands, thinking, "Am I crazy?"

This all happened in the age before cell phones. I had to go back to the office to call her again.

"Oh no, not Apartment B, Apartment *D*," she said.

I drove back over and knocked on Apartment D. No one answered.

I returned to the office, still empty-handed. I couldn't reach her by phone. I had to tell the clients that the report wasn't ready.

When I finally did get a hold of The Bagel Slicer, this is what she had to say: "I was slicing a bagel, and I cut my finger. I had to run to the emergency room."

In the end, she concocted some sort of dog-ate-my-homework excuse for why the report didn't exist. If I remember correctly, it involved some strange, highly unusual computer glitch. It took all the will power I had to resist the temptation to ask The Bagel Slicer to remove the bandage from her hand so that I could see the wound.

The Bagel Slicer taught me an important lesson about Rule #1 people. Many impossible Rule #1 people operate almost exclusively in the present tense. They are concerned only about the one moment in front of them. Their thought processes simply don't stretch forward to encompass any future consequences.

Obviously, The Bagel Slicer hadn't finished the report. Just as obviously, I was going to find out that the report wasn't finished when it didn't arrive in time for the client meeting.

But The Bagel Slicer was looking at this situation according to her own strange logic. She was making decisions focused on increments of time that stretched about five minutes into the future.

Can I survive this phone call without being found out? Can I survive this one knock at the door? Can I survive this next knock at the door?

She never engaged at all with the real problem at hand — namely, that the report wasn't done. The anguish and confusion she was causing me as I chased after her that day probably never entered her mind. All she cared about was getting through that present moment. She had no concern for what might arise further down the road.

4.3 **Lessons from the Cheese Shop**

One of my favorite old Monty Python skits is "The Cheese Shop." It begins when a customer played by John Cleese enters The National Cheese Emporium and finds Michael Palin behind the counter. Randomly, there is a bouzouki player and two dancers performing in the shop.

Cleese asks Palin for a little Red Leicester.

"I'm afraid we're fresh out of Red Leicester, sir."

And with that, they are off and running. Cleese proceeds to ask about 43 different cheeses, and Palin comes up empty handed 43 different times. As he ticks of one cheese after another—including the fictional "Venezuelan Beaver Cheese"—Cleese slowly but surely loses his self-control until, in a pitch-perfect illustration of Rule #1, he starts to lose his mind. At one point he comes completely unglued, dropping F bombs and screaming "SHUT THAT BLOODY BOUZOUKI OFF!"

Finally, Cleese decides that it might be time to apply Rule #4 and Count the Bricks.

"Have you, in fact, got any cheese here at all?"

And that's when Palin is forced to admit that there is no cheese in The Cheese Shop—"not a scrap."

Alas, by the time Cleese finally figures out the question he should have asked long ago, he has gone crazy. He pulls out a gun and shoots the cheese shop owner dead. It's a rather extreme ending for a skit that otherwise might be titled "Rule #1: Crazy Person Makes John Cleese Crazy."

4.4 See It to Believe It

When it came time to Count the Bricks, The Fixer was amazing. Do you remember him from Rule #3? He was the best manager I've ever seen, the guy who my old consulting company would fly in when one of its big multi-million dollar projects was falling apart.

Some of these jobs involved hundreds of people. When projects like that go awry, everyone falls into a state of panic and despair. It's as if they're all flailing their arms around, trying to move while standing in quicksand.

The Fixer would stop everyone in his or her tracks. Quite literally: he would order everyone and everything about the project to shut down.

Then he'd set about counting the bricks. In a series of meetings with key players, The Fixer would focus on understanding the basic facts of the matter—how far along was the project and what still needed doing. He always seemed to have an intuitive grasp of just how many metaphorical bricks any particular piece of a project needed and what colors and sizes they should be.

He refused to allow any Rule #3 FUD or other distractions into these sessions, which would continue for however long it took for The Fixer to get a clear look at the reality buried under all the Rule #1 confusion.

Then he'd simply start slogging away, choosing one piece of the project to focus on first and then slowly adding another and another until at long last everyone involved in the project was back up and running again—no longer stuck in the quicksand.

Most Rule #1 situations aren't that complicated, of course. Most Rule #1 encounters in life involve a single person, like The Bagel Slicer. If I had known about the 90/50 Theory back then, I would have had some pretty good options once I realized it was time to Count the Bricks.

I could have moved her deadline up by a couple of weeks so that I had enough of a cushion to put someone else on the job before the clients arrived. I could have insisted on seeing the draft document that was supposedly 90% done.

The point is that in virtually any Rule #1 situation, there will be some way to measure progress and to protect against problems. The important thing is to step in early and insist on seeing the work and its progress with your own eyes. With Rule #1 people, you can believe it only when you see it.

4.5 *"Doveryai, no Proveryai"*

When the leaders of the United States and the Soviet Union gathered to sign an historic arms treaty in 1987, the occasion involved a surprisingly lighthearted moment.

President Ronald Reagan had once dismissed his treaty partner as an "evil empire." On another occasion, during a sound check when he didn't realize he was in front of a hot microphone, Reagan had joked, "My fellow

Americans, I'm pleased to tell you today that I've signed legislation that will outlaw Russia forever. We begin bombing in five minutes."

But just like Cold Warrior Richard Nixon went to China, so Reagan sat down with the Soviets and reached a deal in the end. The phrase *"Doveryai, no proveryai"* is a Russian proverb Reagan came to know along the way. It means, "Trust, but verify," and Reagan used the phrase over and over.

He used it again at the treaty signing, and this time Soviet Premier Mikhail Gorbachev called him out on it.

"You always say that," Gorbachev said with a laugh.

"I like the sound of it," Reagan replied.

Once you begin to suspect that a Rule #1 situation is at hand, you should adopt that Russian proverb as your own. Don't assume the worst of people while still navigating these warning signs. But be cautious, too, and be ready at every step to Count the Bricks.

Trust, but verify.

4.6 The Bottom Line

Rule #1 people often have a problem with progress reports. The root of this problem lies in their desire to win approval and avoid getting in any trouble. Those goals can take precedence in their minds over the rules of logical thinking and even basic honesty.

As a result, they tend to give progress reports that are divorced from reality. When they say that they are 90 percent done, they are probably not even 50 percent of the way home. It's quite possible that they haven't even started the job.

When you hear a warning sign of this type, it's time to pay close attention to the progress report. It's time to get the potential Rule #1 character to open the books so that you can Count the Bricks and see how far along the progress really is.

Tangent—Playing on the B Team

As we make our way through this book, the importance of maintaining a calm, rational mindset in the face of Rule #1 craziness will become more and more clear. A friend of mine who enjoyed a successful career in carpentry at a big hospital once shared with me a good example of that mindset in action.

Fred had been working at the hospital for 20 years by that point. There were quite a few other "lifers" on staff in his department as well.

Over the years, this hospital kept shaking up its leadership ranks. Fred's department had churned through 10 different managers in his 20 years. Each new manager set out to make his or her own set of changes to the way things worked.

The department got downsized, up-sized, right-sized, and wrong-sized. It whipped through strategic plans in what seemed a matter of months. At one time or another, Fred endured just about every management fad in the health-care field.

The constant turnover created a Rule #1 environment, but Fred and his co-workers seemed to do a great job of keeping things in perspective, not letting the constant barrage of changes make them frustrated or angry.

"We would joke among ourselves about how we should have hats and t-shirts made up identifying us as the B Team," he told me. "And we were the B Team because we were going to *be* there long after this new manager is gone. Our attitude was to just go along with things for a while and wait it out."

FREUDIAN COIN TOSS

Rule #5 - Think Twice About First Impressions

5.0 The Concept

How do you know?

How do you know you know?

You've seen one or more warning signs. You suspect that you might have a Rule #1 situation on your hands. But how do you know for sure?

Rule #1 people do things that can cause the rest of us to behave in crazy ways, which is why here in Rule #5 I will be sharing several strategies designed to make sure that you are thinking about the key question—is this a Rule#1 situation?—in clear, logical fashion and with calm, collected emotions.

5.1 Impossible Means Impossible

There is a word in the subtitle of this book that was not chosen lightly, and that word is *impossible*.

Do you remember the old TV show, "Mission Impossible"? Week after week, it ended with a successful and generally happy turn of events. "Mission *Possible*" might have been a more accurate title.

That is not the case here, and that's why it's so important to understand as early as possible whether you really are in a Rule #1 situation. It's a definitional thing: If the person is impossible, then the situation surrounding that person is also impossible. And if that is the case, then we need to recognize that life is too short to get caught up in the craziness ahead. Instead, we need to get about the work of figuring out the best and most responsible way to step clear of the situation.

As we've seen, Rule #1 people are living mostly on the unmoored side of life's seesaw. They tend to be disconnected from the ways of grounded people when it comes to things as basic as politeness, logic, honesty, and fair play. They are, in short, impossible.

Why am I saying all this here? What I'm hoping to do is encourage you to actually make a decision about whether you are in Rule #1 territory—and to do so in a prompt fashion. It can be tempting to put this sort of is-it-or-is-it-not question to the side for a while. But that would be a mistake. Left unattended, impossible situations always get more impossible.

I remember reading a book a few years ago that set out to teach readers how to succeed in difficult negotiations. The book basically laid out a strategy for putting a win—win deal in front of a difficult person in just the right way and at just the right time, so that he or she had no choice but to see the light and sign on the dotted line.

This is simply not true when Rule #1 comes into play. That book lumped together two very different categories of people—the merely *difficult,* and the truly *impossible.*

This book is about the truly impossible. Rule #1 people will never see the light of your logic. It doesn't matter how long and hard you try to bring them around. You will never understand their logic or reasoning.

That's why it's key to understand as early as you can whether Rule #1 is in effect. Left alone, Rule #1 situations can spin out of control. What follows here are some decision-making strategies that will help you make the call.

5.2 The Head, Heart & Style Evaluation

Rule #1 people come in many different types. They can be introverted, and they can be bombastic. They can be leaders, and they can be followers. They can be comedians, and they can be humorless.

As we saw in Rule #2, they often manage to make a strong first impression. And first impressions can be funny things—they have a tendency to stick in our minds long after we've actually gotten to know someone at a deeper level.

In Rule #1 situations, the danger is that a positive first impression lingers so strongly in the mind that it delays the realization that someone is actually living on the unmoored side of life's seesaw.

At the consulting firm, we were always shuttling into and out of new companies as we moved from one assignment to another. We had a strategy that helped us get settled in to new places—we called it the "instant evaluation system."

It came in handy whenever we had to meet a few dozen people over the course of a couple of days. Invariably, we'd get asked during that time a question along the lines of, "What did you think of Jason?" And this would come after we'd spent a grand total of three or four minutes in Jason's presence.

But our clients wanted an answer and we wanted to make a good impression with them, so we learned to structure our answer by touching on three things: Head, Heart, and Style.

"Oh, Jason seems like a smart guy, with a good grasp of the basics here. Seems like a hard worker, dedicated, and he came off to me as being good with people—that's always important."

There you have it—the instant evaluation.

But with Rule #1 people, that quick first impression is a dangerous thing. It creates a presumption of normality that can be difficult to put aside later on, even in the face of growing evidence. This is one thing that leads people into those Rule #2 moments where they end up questioning their own sanity.

Sometimes it takes a long time to process and accept the fact that there is an impossible Rule #1 person around. Once you become worried about that possibility, it will be important to go back and reevaluate your first impressions. Break out the Head, Heart, and Style evaluation and run it through the wringer of actual experience.

Sure, Jason seemed like a smart guy at first. But is he really making the most logical decisions? Or is it too often a jumble with him—is he too focused on the here and now and not enough on the long-term goals of the project and the company? What about Jason's style? Does he fit in with his colleagues, or does it seem like they tend to keep their distance from him?

Do you remember how Henry, the Rule #1 character from the utility company in Georgia, had that penchant for working late into the night, long after everyone else had gone home? He'd show up late the next morning, looking a little haggard. At first, we thought that looked like the dedication of a hard worker. But as time went on it started to look more and more like showing off by a worker who was more interested in playing the part of a hero than in getting the job done.

In order to make realizations like that, we need to step back and reevaluate.

Based on my experience with Rule #1 people, I have a prediction to make about how those Head, Heart, and Style reevaluations are going to work out. Most of the time when you reevaluate a Rule #1 person using Head, Heart & Style, it won't be the Heart or the Style that come to the forefront. It will be The Head.

That's the category where the positive first impression that Rule #1 people make most often turns out to be a mirage. From their position on the unmoored side of life's seesaw, they are simply not thinking about things in normal ways. They're not following the rules of logic. They're not keeping the big picture of a project or a company in mind.

5.3 The Freudian Coin Toss

If you're in the midst of a tough call concerning a possible Rule #1 situation, try the Freudian Coin Toss.

My wife Katharine learned about the Freudian Coin Toss years ago and found it quite useful when she needed to help our daughters make an important decision.

The idea here is not really to let the coin make a decision, but to get inside the child's heart and identify how she really feels. The coin would go up in the air and come down tails.

Katharine would say, "OK, the coin says tails. How do you feel about that?"

More often than not, the child who couldn't make up her mind suddenly knew what she wanted.

So when you have a decision to make that could go either way, flip the coin and see how you feel about it. By analyzing your reaction, you find that you really know the answer.

Where did the Freudian Coin Toss come from?

Well, there are actually a lot of references, particularly among motivational speaker types, who have said that it dates straight back to Sigmund Freud himself. In citation after citation, folks write that that Freud sometimes surprised people struggling to make decisions in life with a suggestion that they flip a coin. Then Freud would say (in quotes), "Then look into your own reactions. Ask yourself: Am I pleased? Am I disappointed?"

The exact quote is all over the net. When I set out to find an actual book, article or speech by or about Freud that contains such a quote, I came up empty. I think the chances are good that Freud never said any such thing.

However, that doesn't mean the Freudian Coin Toss is not a good process. You might be surprised at how effective it is particularly in subjective areas like Rule #1.

5.4 Occam's Razor

William of Occam led quite an eventful life, one full of heresy trials and house detentions and even excommunication. The English Franciscan friar is generally regarded as one of the great thinkers of the Middle Ages.

He is remembered today primarily for Occam's Razor, an evaluation tool that's used to make an educated guess about which of several hypotheses is the most likely to be true. An example often cited to explain how the razor works is crop circles.

These large and mysterious circles in fields of wheat were a hot topic back in the 1970s and 1980s. Many people argued that they must be markings made by alien spacecraft landing on Earth. Others scoffed, saying that the circles must be a manmade phenomenon.

Occam's razor says that when looking at two or more hypotheses like these, the one most likely to be correct is the one that has the fewest complicated parts and ideas. The razor turned out to be quite correct in this case, as a couple of guys in England eventually came forward and admitted that it was all a big practical joke.

Occam's razor can come in quite handy in Rule #1 situations. Evaluate your Rule #1 suspicions with an eye towards seeing which is the simplest explanation for how those suspicions came up. If a pattern of irrational, unhinged behavior comes out on top, you'll know it's time to start protecting yourself from the Rule #1 rain.

5.5 The Obvious Test

A former colleague of mine from the consulting firm eventually moved on to a software development firm. When we got together one evening a few years ago, he told me the story of a recent adventure he had while hiring a network engineer.

The process had nearly run its course. Everything was going quite smoothly. The top candidate had come to the company's attention through a trusted headhunter. He had passed his background check. My former colleague and his hiring team were about to make an offer.

But that company had a smart policy in place. After a few bad hiring experiences over the years, they adopted a practice of always conducting an online screening of potential hires. They would take a look at their Facebook page and other social media activity. They would Google the person's name.

It seems so simple, right? What are the chances of anything popping up?

When my colleague Googled the name of this particular top candidate, what popped up was an outstanding recent charge of attempted murder, something involving an ex-wife and her new beau and a gun going off. It was right there on the front page of the local newspaper for the town where he lived.

Rule #1 situations are, by definition, crazy ones. They can become convoluted affairs, full of surprising twists and turns that make it hard to see the forest for the trees. The Obvious Test encourages you to take a step back from all those complexities and focus on sources of simple, straightforward information.

When it comes time to make a decision about a potential Rule #1 situation, ask yourself this question: What is the easiest, simplest way to check on that? Often, the answers delivered by The Obvious Test will turn out to be much more revealing than expected.

5.6 The Bottom Line

How do you know? The truth is, there may be uncertainties as you try to evaluate whether a situation is Rule #1, or not. And while the tests outlined here in Rule #5 will help you make that determination, they may not eliminate every last doubt.

It's important to remember that false negatives are worse than false positives. If you mistakenly decide that a Rule #1 person is not, in fact, crazy, that will be a much more costly mistake than deciding that a sensible person is, in fact, crazy.

The latter mistake will generally work itself out over time, but the former mistake will often amount to a major setback that could end up costing you a lot of time and emotional energy.

Tangent—The First Rule of Lifesaving

Anytime Rule #1 arises, there is a risk that we ourselves will lose our way. As we've seen throughout this book, Rule #1 people can make *you* behave in crazy ways. Rule #1 situations have an undertow-like quality to them, a way of drawing you deeper into the depths of the craziness at hand.

Did you know that in the world of lifesaving, they have their own Rule #1? It's "Don't let yourself drown."

There is nothing tongue-in-cheek about this first rule of lifesaving. People who fear they might be drowning are desperate and highly dangerous. While flailing about wildly, they are perfectly capable of knocking you unconscious. They will almost certainly try to climb on top of you and then stay there in order to save themselves.

Here is the sequence they teach in lifeguard school: "Throw, Row, Go." The first strategy you try is to throw a lifeline towards a drowning person. The second strategy is to row up to them in a boat. The third choice, swimming up to them, is only to be used as a last resort.

When things go badly for Rule #1 people, they often behave in ways that make them dangerous in the same way those drowning people are dangerous. They try to drag others into the situation. They turn to new and deeper levels of Rule #1 behavior. They can make wild accusations and tell infuriating fibs.

One key goal of this book is helping you stay clear of this Rule #1 undertow. If and when things get really, really out of hand in your Rule #1 situation, remember the first rule of lifesaving and be sure to keep your distance.

THE FARMER AND THE SNAKE.

Rule #6 - Trouble Now Is Trouble Later

6.0 The Concept

Dealing with impossible people is hard. It's likely to involve difficult encounters and perhaps some unpleasant exchanges. There is no getting around this. But the temptation to put that hard work aside until next week, or next month, must be avoided.

We want to think the best of people. We keep hoping that they will come through for the team. We keep thinking that by next time they will have learned from their mistakes. With Rule #1 people, that amounts to wishful thinking.

Once Rule #1 is in play, the problems are going to get worse going forward, not better. Dealing with them is going to be even harder down the road than it is at the moment. The time to take action is now.

6.1 The Farmer and the Snake

Here is a parable to keep in mind as you come to grips with the fact that you have a Rule #1 situation on your hands.

A farmer was riding home on his tractor down the dirt road one cold winter day when he spotted a snake that looked to be in big trouble. It had been run over by a car. It couldn't move. It was freezing. It was going to be stuck there on the pavement, until it starved, froze, or got run over again.

The farmer took pity on the poor snake. He picked him up and took him home. He crafted a cozy little box nest for the snake and set it by a warm fire. The farmer fed and cared for the snake every day for months. Over time, he came to love having the snake around. By springtime, the snake was healthy again.

One day, as the spring sun warmed up the room, the farmer leaned down to pet his friend. The snake jumped up and bit him. The farmer was poisoned. He was going to die.

"Snake, after all I've done for you, nursing you back to health and feeding you and befriending you, how could you bite me like that? And now you're going to leave me here to die?"

The snake looked at the farmer for a long second.

The snake said, "You knew I was a snake, right?"

A snake is a snake. No amount of care and kindness will stop it from behaving like a snake. So it is with Rule #1 people. They are crazy today, and they will be crazy tomorrow as well. There are times in life when we are powerless to change the basic nature of things. This is one of those times.

6.2 The One-Way Phenomenon

The inclination to be generous and helpful comes naturally to most people. When a co-worker messes up, our first instinct is to give her a second chance. When a colleague is struggling with a task, we try to connect him with the training he needs.

In most areas of life and work, these instincts are right on the money. They help to generate an atmosphere of trust and foster a spirit of camaraderie in the workplace. They form the foundation for the unwritten rules of civil society governing our sense of reciprocity and our concept of fair play.

When an impossible person enters the picture, however, these natural instincts are no longer right on the money. In fact, they are dead wrong. The rule to remember here is, "Trouble Now Is Trouble Later."

Rule #1 people do not play by the rules of civil society. They don't feel a sense of loyalty towards someone who gives them a second chance. They don't feel gratitude when someone reaches out with a helping hand.

In their strange world, all emotional obligation travels in one and only one direction. It's other people who owe the Rule #1 person loyalty and gratitude. It's never the other way around.

Recognizing this will be a key part of the attitude adjustment that's required when Rule #1 comes into play. No longer will the natural instincts towards generosity and helpfulness be of any use.

Not only will reaching out with a helping hand likely accomplish nothing, it might even make matters worse. Such offers can exacerbate an impossible person's sense of emotional entitlement. In Rule #1 situations, it's best to put some of our most natural instincts aside.

6.3 The Mack Truck Theory

When I was at the consulting firm, I went through a management-training program called Model-Netics. It was the brainchild of Harold Hook, the former CEO of the life insurance company American General. To summarize it broadly, Model-Netics involves seeing new problems and challenges through the lens of one or another of a couple of hundred different "model" situations we were all supposed to commit to memory.

One of those scenarios has special resonance in the Rule #1 world. It's called "The Mack Truck Theory." We even had a little truck icon to remind us of how important this rule is. It goes like this: If there is someone on your team who is so indispensable that your whole project would fall apart if he or she got hit by a truck, well, you need to do something about that. Immediately.

As we've seen with our friend Henry in Atlanta, there is a certain type of Rule #1 person who loves to play the role of a Mack Truck hero. They long to be the person everyone is depending on to save the day—that's where they find emotional satisfaction in life.

There are two problems with this. The first is that in order to finagle themselves into position to play this role, these Rule #1 characters become expert knowledge hoarders. They create little fiefdoms inside of a company or a project where they become the only person who holds the key that will unlock a crisis.

These would-be heroes aren't necessarily restricted to technology jobs, like the one Henry had in Atlanta. Knowledge hoarders might also be on the sales staff, where they jealously guard all access to and information about one of the company's biggest and best customers. They might be in a school system, keeping track of the financial books in some one-of-a-kind way that makes him or her the only one in the system who knows how much money there is left in the budget.

In cases like these, there will almost certainly be no current documentation of the duties, workflow, and processes of these Rule #1 people. More often than not, they'll have strong relationships with upper managers and principals, so much so that any attempt to insist on a fix for the documentation problem will be greeted with resistance.

"Oh, Jane's too important to us right now," the boss will say. "We don't want to force all this extra documentation work on her—it'll just cause trouble. Leave it alone for now."

In addition to the fact that knowledge hoarding can be a difficult problem to fix, there is a second problem that arises when both The Mack Truck Theory and Rule #1 are in play at the same time. There's a term in the investing world called "alignment of interests," which is used to describe the ethical way of structuring relationships, so that a brokerage firm, an individual broker, and an investor all share the same goals. It's about making sure that what's good for the firm is good for the broker and also for the investor.

The Rule #1 people who put themselves into Mack Truck positions are almost always out of alignment with the company's goals. They are highly motivated to leave a crisis unresolved for as long as they can remain the center of attention, rather than resolving it in a timely, efficient way. This is, after all, where they get their emotional juice in life.

6.4 Bob's Corollary

My friend Bob has been a big fan of this whole Rule #1 concept over the years. Whenever we get together, he's always urging me to stop talking about the book and finish writing it already.

Whenever we're out in public together, he explains the idea to everyone within earshot. But he never remembers the words of Rule #1 correctly. No matter how many times I correct him, Bob insists on calling it, "Rule #1: Crazy people do crazy things."

Here in Rule #6, however, perhaps I should concede that Bob has a point. That is what we're saying here, isn't it? Crazy people are going to do crazy things, and they are going to keep doing crazy things. That's what happens to people who live life on the unmoored side of life's seesaw. No amount of logical talk from other people is going to change that.

Rule #1 people can come in to work each new morning and somehow forget or ignore all of the discussions they had with you yesterday. When you try to talk things out with them as if they were on the grounded side of the seesaw, they will win that battle. If you plead with them out of a sense of friendship and loyalty, they will toss that friendship aside.

They want different things out of the workplace—and out of life—than the rest of us.

When it comes to impossible people, we need to stop trying to fix things by showing them the error of their ways. Going down that road may be our first instinct, but it's only going to end in some mind-boggling new version of "Groundhog Day," in which we are stuck in place, failing day after day after day to make any progress. Life is too short. We don't have time for long Rule #1 detours.

So Bob is right: Crazy people do crazy things. And they're going to continue to do crazy things in the coming days, weeks, and months.

6.5 "We wouldn't want to hold you back."

Is there anything you can do when you have a Rule #1 person at the wheel, driving your project or team down the road at a high speed? How do you manage to take away the keys and make the transition to a new driver?

One of our client companies from my consulting days had a Rule #1 character named William. William was the kind of guy who was always pitching one bold new venture or another. He always wanted to take the company off into a new market or a new niche where great riches were waiting to be won.

Like so many Rule #1 people, he was generally able to make a strong first impression. William's enthusiasm for his schemes was quite genuine—and could be contagious to boot. He gave great presentations. He had genuinely creative ideas.

He was actually very popular with most of the company's top managers.

In time, however, it became apparent to his boss that William was definitely Rule #1. To make matters worse, his interests and motivations were badly out of alignment with the company's goals. William loved being in on the ground floor of big new projects. He got his emotional satisfaction at the point in the race where the starting gate flips open and everyone is off and running.

But he wasn't really interested in running the whole race. How a project turned out over the long haul didn't matter much to William. By that point, he'd be off feeding his emotional appetite at some other starting gate, where he was launching another big new project.

William's big ideas usually flamed out and failed in the end. But by the time that happened, he was long gone and working on something else. Someone else would be in charge, and they would end up with the blame for the failure of William's concept.

This particular company put a high value on longevity and experience. When a senior person came in and announced that she was considering a job offer, we almost always did our best to sweeten the pot and keep her in the fold.

Almost always. One day William came in to see his boss and announced that he had received an offer from a company in California. He told his boss that he was flattered by the offer—and by the salary increase on the table—but that he was of course dedicated to the project in front of him at the client company. He was hoping to work something out with his boss.

This boss understood Rule #1 situations. He saw the opportunity in front of him, and he seized it, telling William that the new offer sounded perfect for him and that he could not bring himself to try and talk William out of accepting it.

He reached out his hand in a congratulatory gesture and said, "We wouldn't want to hold you back, William—you deserve this. We're all happy for you, and we wish the best of luck to you."

That boss got lucky with William. But I learned something important from observing that episode. In Rule #1 situations, you need to always have your eyes open, ready to recognize opportunities that present a pain-free way of moving Rule #1 people away from your projects and from your workplace--ideally, into a position where they will not be able to cause much damage.

I call it the "We wouldn't want to hold you back" strategy as a tribute to William.

Remember, these people tend to have big egos. They often think they can put the weight of the world on their shoulders. They regard themselves as indispensable, and they often think they don't get the credit they deserve.

Smart managers will try to come up with creative ways to use these tendencies to their advantage. A colleague of mine in the insurance industry told me once about the day a Rule #1 person came into her office saying something about how he should be given more responsibilities, and perhaps a promotion.

My colleague turned that conversation into a gentle push towards the door.

"I do understand what you're saying," she told him, "but we're a small team here and we don't have much turnover. It's hard to imagine that the kind of promotion you want will ever come available. Have you thought about checking in with human resources? Maybe there is an opportunity somewhere else in the company that would be a better fit for you. I don't want you to feel like you're trapped here when my hands are tied and I'm unable to offer you that promotion."

Let me close here with a postscript about William. Once he left that client company, his old boss followed the path of his career through the industry grapevine. He took that job in California, of course, and there he launched a gigantic new initiative that sounded swell, but failed spectacularly after a few years. William wasn't around for the failure, of course. But that time he was 1,500 miles away, working with yet a new company on yet another big project launch.

6.6 The Bottom Line

When Rule #1 situations first arise, a strong temptation will arise to ignore it for a while, or to just work around it temporarily. It's an understandable temptation. These situations are not easy. They require acting with courage, smarts, and discipline. They involve having exchanges with people that are bound to be difficult.

But it's critical to resist that temptation to go into avoidance mode. More often than not, trouble now is not just trouble later—it's *more* trouble later and then *even more* trouble after that. Setting the issue aside at the outset is only going to make it that much more complicated and confusing down the road. Remember: life is too short to allow yourself to get caught up in that.

Carpe diem. Once you recognize a Rule #1 situation, it's time to seize the day and take action now to try and shelter yourself and your workplace colleagues from the Rule #1 rain.

Tangent – Get off at Exit Ramps

My father taught me a lasting lesson about the right way to make decisions in life's more stressful moments. I went to college in Milwaukee, and one semester there everything went south for me. I hated my living arrangements. I didn't like my classes.

One day in the middle of a semester, I decided that I'd had enough. I packed up my things, arranged a ride to the airport, and got on a flight to Philadelphia. From there I called and asked my dad for a ride home to a nearby suburb.

When we sat down in the living room, he asked to hear my story. After I told him, my dad was quiet for a long stretch of time. When he finally spoke, he said a wise thing.

"You know when you're traveling down the highway and it comes time to get off because you've gone far enough? The safe thing to do in that situation is to wait until there's an exit ramp and take the exit ramp. Don't just turn the wheel to the right whenever you're feeling the need to get off."

I went back to Milwaukee, thinking I'd finish out that semester and then quit. But then things started to get a little better with my living arrangements and my classes, and I ended up sticking around and earning my diploma. Thanks, Dad.

In your encounters with Rule #1 people, it's quite possible that things will get so bad that you will be tempted to walk away. Don't allow yourself to do anything rash and permanent in such moments.

Instead, take your time and watch for exit ramps up ahead. Is there a promotion you can apply for, or a transfer to a new department you can request? Is it time to seek a new job with a different firm? Or perhaps the exit ramp will take the form of arranging a transfer for the Rule #1 person, one designed to keep him from causing so much trouble.

Here, too, a little patience usually pays dividends.

Rule #7 - If It Feels Good, Don't Say It

7.0 The Concept

Maintaining a calm, rational mindset is a key to coping more effectively with Rule #1 people. This sounds easier than it is. Out in the real world, Rule #1 people behave in ways that can be supremely frustrating and even offensive. Their illogical behavior can set your work on a project back by weeks or months. Living on the unmoored side of life's seesaw, they often lack basic social graces and can seem rude and uncaring as a result.

Self-restraint is key. If you lose control in a Rule #1 situation, you will make things worse, not better. Groucho Marx once observed, "If you speak when angry, you'll make the best speech you'll ever regret." Don't do it. Resist the urge.

7.1 The Heroine Syndrome

The starting point of this book way back at the beginning is that Rule #1 situations can take a person who is accustomed to living on the grounded end of life's seesaw and drive them crazy, to the point where they themselves end up sitting on the unmoored side of the seesaw, struggling with some powerful emotions—anger, frustration, and even betrayal.

In most cases, Rule #1 people don't set out on purpose to leave other people feeling like that. More likely, they are simply unaware of the fact that they can drive people crazy with their twisted logic and unreliable memories.

For you, the temptation to vent in such stressful situations will be very strong. But it needs to be resisted, especially while in the presence of the Rule #1 character at hand. Be warned that this is likely to take a lot of internal fortitude. It's not going to be easy.

My friend JoAnn told me a story recently about how she gave into that temptation once—and about how it made things worse, not better. The nonprofit group she leads was helping organize a public art project in the small town where she lives. The artist she was working with was quite talented, but she was also Rule #1 through and through.

This artist had a heroine complex. In fact, let's call her The Heroine. She thought it was her destiny to put this struggling little town on her back and carry it to greatness by virtue of the inspirational magic of her visionary artworks.

The Heroine couldn't be bothered with mundane things like the invoices and receipts JoAnn needed to keep the grant funds flowing. She blew past every reporting deadline. When her expense reports finally arrived, they were incomprehensible.

Whenever JoAnn tried to show The Heroine what a proper report looked like, she would respond with nods and assurances. Then the next report would come in looking even more pathetic than the last one.

Eventually, as JoAnn had repeatedly warned, all the missing and incomplete reports caused funding for the project to be suspended because of paperwork problems. This, of course, is the moment when The Heroine began badmouthing JoAnn and her charity all around town.

Along the way, JoAnn caught The Heroine telling a big public lie about the contractual agreement she'd made to work on the project. Furious, JoAnn confronted The Heroine. She told her exactly what she thought of her behavior. She didn't do it rudely, or publicly, but she called The Heroine out to her face, and it felt awfully good.

Then JoAnn saw the expression on The Heroine's face. And immediately, she knew that she had just made an even bigger mess of things. The Heroine was mystified by JoAnn's criticism—as incomprehensible as it seem to JoAnn, The Heroine had no idea what JoAnn was talking about.

Worse still, the artist now had a fresh supply of Rule #1 energy—now she would get to play martyr as well as heroine. In the end, it didn't matter one bit that JoAnn was right about that lie or that The Heroine deserved a tongue-lashing. All JoAnn succeeded in doing was to make a crazy situation crazier.

The moral of JoAnn's story, then, is Rule #7: "If it feels good, don't say it."

7.2 "Fine" Is a Four-Letter Word

In situations that are frustrating and difficult, it's human nature to look for ways to release bottled-up emotions. Rule #1 situations are often filled with such frustrations, of course, and that makes this particular instinct a dangerous one to indulge around impossible people.

It can lead to voices rising in anger and accusations flying this way and that. That's not likely to lead to a productive outcome.

But still there may come a need for venting. In those occasions, there is one four-letter word that's allowed: *Fine.*

When uttered in Rule #1 situations, it should sound like the very last word in a long and passionate argument. It should be spoken through clenched teeth, with enough oomph behind the *f* sound to make it seem like every last bit of frustration is being blown out of the body.

This really does work. It offers a sense of physical release, while still keeping the risks of escalating a situation to a minimum.

I had occasion to share this strategy with one of my colleagues at one company where I worked. After he received a promotion to vice president of service, George spent about five years reporting to me when I was chief operating officer. Week in and week out, I saw the diligent and dedicated way he went about the work of trying to build a good department into a great one.

Then we had some turnover in the executive ranks, which caused a bit of a leadership shuffle. George was now set to take on a different senior role in the organization. He was also assigned to continue working in service for the next six months as the new leadership there came aboard.

Over the course of his five years, George had taken that department through a detailed visioning process. He had brought in new equipment, added new trainings, and instituted new protocols.

"We've made so much progress," he told me one day. "But we're not done turning that vision into reality. There are still some steps that need to be taken to finish what we started."

The problem was, the new leadership in the department wasn't really interested in taking those final steps that George saw as so critical to finishing the job. Instead, they wanted to back up by five years and start back at square one with a new visioning process. It was a natural outcome of a change in leadership.

I sympathized with George. I'd watched him put his heart and soul into developing and implementing that vision for the department, and I could tell he was having an extremely difficult time with this turn of events.

After it was all over, he stopped by to thank me for sharing my "Fine is a four-letter word" strategy with him. He said he found it quite helpful in finally and fully letting go of his old position so that he could stop looking back and step into a new role.

"Saying that out loud, it was about freeing myself from worry and concern over something that I really just didn't control anymore," George said. After getting in his last four-letter word, he asked for and then received the opportunity to cut short his six-month stay in the service area and devote all his attention to his new post.

That wasn't a Rule #1 situation, strictly speaking. There weren't any crazy people in the mix that I am aware of. But the principle is the same. George had to find a way to release the frustrations that were piling up inside, and *"fine!"* helped him do just that.

7.3 Walking up to Sheep

One of the truly precious things in our family's life together has been the little farm we've called home for a long time now. It's set among some gorgeous rolling hills in the Maryland countryside.

Growing up, our two daughters were enthusiastic 4-H kids. They wanted the opportunity to raise animals to show at the county and state fairs, and their mother and I were more than happy to oblige.

We ended up with a small flock of sheep. Twenty head was probably the biggest it ever got. The sheep themselves were quite big. A mature ram in the breed that we brought in can weigh between 175 and 275 pounds. Ewes weigh in at between 130 and 180.

We learned quite a few sheep-tending tricks along the way. One of them involves a bit of trickery when it's time for shearing or some other bit of business that the sheep isn't really fond of.

You never, ever walk straight at a sheep. They'll sense something is up, and they'll bolt. To make matters worse, the sheep will then be on high alert for the rest of the day, running away any time you come within a mile of them.

What you want to do instead is walk in the general direction of the sheep, but off line, as if your final destination is not the sheep at all, but a tree up ahead and to the left of where the sheep is standing. Sensing you're going somewhere else, the sheep will relax.

You really don't have to go very far off line to lull them into this relaxed state. You can walk so close that you'll basically be able to just lean over at the last second and grab them.

In this respect at least, Rule #1 people can behave quite a bit like our oversized sheep. It's best to avoid the direct approach with them. Being honest and up front may well be the way to go in most normal circumstances, but normal people will behave in normal ways. They'll recognize their mistakes. They'll feel motivated to correct them.

That's not the case with Rule #1 people. They speak a different emotional language than the rest of us, which is how they can sometimes take an up-front approach from a boss or co-worker and spin it into some big affront to their dignity. The other thing to remember here is that many Rule #1 people go into fight-or-flight mode at the first sign of criticism. Much like our sheep at the farm, they will become even more difficult to handle while in that mode of high alert.

7.4 "Thanksgiving is on a Thursday"

When I think of model behavior in keeping your cool and staying true to Rule #7, I think about a Jesuit priest I met at a luncheon at Loyola University in Baltimore. I found the story of his life to be so fascinating that I kept peppering him with questions through the entire event.

He had two doctorate degrees—one in history and one in English literature. As a Jesuit, he knew his share of both Latin and Greek. He came originally from Goa, a city that's now in India but for centuries was a separate city-state under the control of Portugal. Like many people from Goa, this guy could speak Portuguese as well as a couple of the many different languages spoken in India.

At some point in our afternoon together, the priest told me that he had just recently become an American citizen. I asked him what the experience was like, and he smiled through the entire story that followed.

Once he arrived at the government office where the ceremony was scheduled, the priest had to wait in line for a while and then pick up a number of different forms to fill out. Then he had to wait in several more lines, one for each of the forms that he had filled out. They stamped this one, and they signed that one, and they filed some other ones. It went on and on, the priest said.

Finally, he came to his last stop before the auditorium where he would finally be able to raise his right hand and take the Oath of Allegiance. Standing behind a counter was a pair of government bureaucrats whose job, apparently, was to make sure the applicants could speak some English.

I wasn't there, so I cannot say whether these two bureaucrats are Rule #1 people or not. I would guess that they are not. Sometimes, Rule #1 situations arise because organizations adopt crazy procedures and rules, and the illogical-seeming things that otherwise normal people in those organizations do is the result. This phenomenon seems to be especially common in large government bureaucracies.

In any case, these two men obviously had no actual interest in the diminutive man now standing before them. While he was feeling so eager to move forward and experience one of the most important days of his life, they had a glassy, bored look about them.

After glancing at the priest's remaining paperwork, one of the two employees looked at him and said, "Say these words after me: *'Thanksgiving is on a Thursday.'*"

Think about how many languages my Jesuit friend knows. Think about his multiple doctoral degrees and his fascinating life story. Think about how overjoyed and proud the United States should be to welcome a man like this into the citizenship fold.

As he told me this story, I couldn't believe that his journey to U.S. citizenship could possibly include such an offensive, insulting interlude! If I had been in his shoes, I probably would have said something quite snippy. In fact, I might have opted to recite some Shakespeare.

But my Jesuit friend did nothing of the kind. He opted to find and savor a bit of humor in a situation where others might have taken deep offense. He smiled at the two men and said, quite humbly, "Thanksgiving is on a Thursday."

He kept his eye on the prize. He didn't let a little bureaucratic Rule #1 rain get in the way of his big day. A few minutes later, he experienced at long last the joy of becoming a U.S. citizen.

Remember my Jesuit friend the next time a Rule #1 situation has you ready to blow your stack in frustration. Take a deep breath and repeat this bit of wisdom: "Thanksgiving is on a Thursday." It might help you, too, keep your eyes on the prize.

7.5 Major Positions of Minor Authority

You will find Rule #1 people working in just about any organization of some significant size. Such people often gravitate towards jobs that allow them to occupy what a doctor friend of mine calls "Major Positions of Minor Authority." This type of Rule #1 person tends to be a stickler for rules, no matter how tiny and inconsequential they might be.

Do you remember JoAnn, who runs a nonprofit group in a small town and had to deal with that Rule #1 character called The Heroine? She told me a story about her encounters with the people in the accounting office of her local city government who occupied a couple of these Major Positions of Minor Authority.

For whatever reason, some government grants doled out by the state need to be routed through a local government on their way to a nonprofit group. What this meant for JoAnn is that she was required in turn to route all of her reports and questions about a state-financed project through a city government that really had nothing whatsoever to do with the project beyond shuffling paper.

These grant projects are often long-term affairs. JoAnn would apply for a grant one year, she would receive it the next, and then the project might continue running for four or five years after that. A lot can change over the course of six or seven years. Sometimes JoAnn found herself in need of some flexibility to address changing conditions in her town as those years went by.

These two city employees in the accounting office would have none of it. Any time JoAnn mentioned the possibility of making some little change in the rules governing the grant, they reacted with abject panic. They kept insisting that no changes were allowed, ever, under any circumstances. The only option available was to follow the letter of the original grant agreement.

"Otherwise, we will get in all kinds of trouble with the state, and you will not be allowed access to grants like this ever again," they said.

Then one day JoAnn found herself at an end-of-day conference reception, small talking over a glass of wine with a state grant manager. She asked that manager why the grants she managed had zero flexibility to make the adjustments she needed.

"What are you talking about?" the grant manager said. "We make adjustments like that all the time—all you have to do is let us know, write a memo. Nine times out of ten, it'll be fine. We'll just work up some amendments, and you'll be good to go."

From that moment on, JoAnn always went over the heads of city employees when she needed flexibility on a grant. She would get state approval first, wait for all the paperwork to be complete, and then she would submit the amendments to the city. The city workers were none too happy about this, but JoAnn always tried to handle her encounters with them in such a respectful and polite manner so that the city employees couldn't really find anything to complain about.

Often, there is no reason to stay and fight with a Rule #1 character who is throwing roadblocks in your path from a Major Position of Minor Authority. Look instead for a way around that position that will let you accomplish your goals and steer clear of the Rule #1 rain.

7.6 The Bottom Line

Coping with Rule #1 situations often requires uncommon levels of self-restraint. In the heat of the moment when Rule #1 is in play, we will sometimes find ourselves at the end of our rope, feeling a mix of anger and frustration that builds to the point where we are ready to blow.

That is the moment to take heed of Rule #7. It's time to keep your eye on the prize and remember that blowing up is going to make things worse, not better. If needed, allow yourself a moment of release, but choose that moment wisely—make sure it's not going to heightening any Rule #1 tensions.

Tangent - The Lifespan of Angry Words

My wife has a favorite saying that fits the bill here: "A spoken word is the one thing you can never take back."

We always assumed this bit of wisdom was something she'd picked up as a youngster at the knee of one Irish grandparent or another. But when I went in search of the origin of the phrase, the path led to ancient times in the Middle East.

Here is a fuller version of the aphorism, which is usually attributed to a 7th century Muslim caliph named Omar ibn al-Halif: "Four things come not back: the spoken word; the spent arrow; the past life; the neglected opportunity."

Rule 8 - First Guy on Paper Wins

8.0 The Concept

Living as they do on the unmoored side of life's seesaw, Rule #1 people often have only a tenuous grasp of day-to-day reality. They will sometimes insist you said things that you never said. Other times, they might recall with certainty events that never really happened.

Rule #8 is about the importance of keeping proper documentation when dealing with people who have trouble keeping facts straight. The goal here is to emulate this wonderful bit of Rule #1 wisdom from Winston Churchill: "History will be kind to me for I intend to write it."

When Rule #1 situations get messy—and they almost invariably do, to one degree or another—they can lead to all sorts of complications, from missed deadlines to rocky launches and personnel issues. By taking just a few minutes along the way to create a paper trail that is brief and to the point, you will make the Rule #1 rain in your life much easier to endure.

8.1 Putting a Name on the New World

Perhaps you remember learning in school about Amerigo Vespucci? He was a European explorer who sailed about in the far reaches of the Atlantic Ocean in the wake of the voyages of the much more famous Christopher Columbus.

Vespucci didn't discover anything important. By all logic, the new lands should have been named after Columbus—or, perhaps more accurately, after some Viking chieftain from a few centuries before Columbus.

The reason why they are called the Americas is that Vespucci was the First Guy on Paper. He wrote two letters back home in which he made it clear that the discoveries of his fellow explorers were indeed "New Worlds" and not the easternmost edge of Asia, which is what everyone expected to find at the end of the Atlantic Ocean.

The historical details here are a little dicey. There are some historians who claim that these letters were not written by Vespucci at all, but by someone else who forged his name. There are others who claim that Vespucci may indeed have written the letters, but that they contained some rather gross exaggerations of his accomplishments.

The true and false here is all a little hazy then, just like it is so often in Rule #1 situations. What we do know for sure is that a mapmaker named Martin Waldseemuller heard about those letters and believed them to be genuine. That's how he came to take the Latinized version of Vespucci's first name, Americus, and give it the feminine form of America when he drew a map of the New World in 1507.

Vespucci died in 1512. It's not clear that he was even aware during his lifetime that Waldseemuller had christened the New World in his honor. But his name was the first one on paper, and that's how come he won the naming rights to a pair of continents.

8.2 Why the Paper Trail Matters

Why is it important to be the First Guy on Paper? One obvious reason is that many Rule #1 people have faulty memories. Such behavior is more unintentional than willful on their part, but that doesn't change the fact that Rule #1 people sometimes forget things they promised to do and go off on tangents instead of following a plan.

The sort of paper trail we are talking about here is not long and detailed. No one has time to write up lengthy, blow-by-blow diary entries at the end of every workday. But you should take a few seconds to jot down and then share a few bullet points now and again with the relevant people in the situation.

Let's say, for instance, that you have a meeting with someone you suspect has Rule #1 tendencies. You were going over a problem that has cropped up, and you agreed on a couple of steps to take next. In that case, take a minute to send a friendly message that begins, "Just checking to make sure we're on the same page about next steps ..."

It could be an email. It could be a short memo. These messages might also be employed after meetings where a new project is launched, an important problem is addressed, or a change is made in strategy. In most cases the notes should be bare bones, about the size of a Power Point slide.

Just this modest bit of record keeping will put you on the high ground if and when things get complicated in your Rule #1 situation. You will be the keeper of the record — what happened when, and why.

This sort of short paper trail is a very important piece of Rule #1 rain gear. It helps you take on the role of the calm, rational person who is going to emerge from the storm with his or her reputation intact.

It may seem like I am writing here from a manager's perspective, but that is not the case at all. It will be just as important to follow Rule #8 when it's a boss or manager who is the Rule #1 character. Your paper trail will be an effective defense against any attempt by the boss to deflect blame from himself towards someone or something else. As a member of that person's team, there should be nothing to stop you from being the keeper of the paper trail.

8.3 The Man with the Plans

A few years back, as a big recession took hold, the U.S. government set out in search of "shovel-ready" projects that they could finance right away in an effort to boost the economy. Such all-ready-to-go jobs proved much more difficult to find than anyone had expected, and the whole push turned into a bit of a flop.

Actually, the government had tried the same trick 70 some years before in the Great Depression. But when President Franklin D. Roosevelt went looking for shovel-ready projects, there was a young urban planner in New York City who had all kinds of proposals ready to go if a sudden influx of New Deal tax dollars and Civilian Conservation Corps workers were to suddenly materialize.

His name was Robert Moses. Moses was always determined to get everything on paper. Throughout his long career, he was constantly busy developing new blueprints and work plans and cost estimates for parks, highways, bridges, and other public works.

Known as "the master builder," he was a rare combination—a visionary on the ideas side, but also someone who understood how to work the levers of power within a government bureaucracy better than anyone else.

Moses wasn't really working in a Rule #1 environment, per se, but his approach remains a great example of how getting things on paper before anyone else does puts you in a position to move quickly and control the agenda. Being the first guy on paper was a key to Moses' success. Whenever a government official went looking for ideas for civic improvements or responses to civic problems, there was Moses, picking up one of his ready-to-go plans, dusting it off, and presenting it—all in the blink of an eye.

Meanwhile, everyone else who wanted to get in on the action was stuck back at the starting gate. They were still brainstorming potential ideas. They had no plans on paper, no costs estimates ready, and no visible evidence that they were even remotely "shovel ready."

How well did being the First Guy on Paper work out for Moses? By the time his career wound down in the 1960s, he had built 150,000 housing units, 658 playgrounds, 416 miles of parkways, and 13 bridges in New York City. In today's dollars, that's a staggering $150 billion worth of work.

It's a little different in Rule #1 situations, of course. Remember, our goal here is not winning glory in posterity on a Moses-like level. Rather, it's simply to cope better in Rule #1 situations by taking the proactive step of jotting down and sharing important plans and decisions as they get made. That puts you in position to be the one who can document what happened when.

8.4 Coloring Books for Executives

I had to give an important presentation to a roomful of CEO-level executives in the insurance industry a few years ago. I worked incredibly hard putting that presentation together. I was convinced that I had some very important points to share, and I decided when putting things together that the CEOs should see every step of logic and calculation I took on the way to my conclusions.

The presentation was a disaster. I got so caught up in detailing all of my brilliant calculations that I lost track of time. All of a sudden one of the CEOs announced that we had run out of time. He thanked me for my presentation and shuffled me out of the room to tepid applause.

I never even got out of the weeds. I hadn't reached the part of the presentation where I revealed the conclusions that I thought were so important.

A few months later, I told this sad story to a colleague, and she is the one who introduced me to the concept of Coloring Books for Executives. The basic idea is this:

When communicating with high-powered executives, you need to keep things as simple and straightforward as possible.

Don't take them blow by blow through a lengthy story. Don't take them step by step through your thinking process. Start with your conclusions. The very first thing you say should be the most important thing. You can work back through all the history of the situation later, if needed.

What does this have to do with Rule #8? We've seen how important it is to be the first guy on paper, but it's also important to communicate effectively on that paper. By keeping Coloring Books for Executives in mind, you'll stay focused on the bottom line issues.

I once heard someone criticize "Coloring Books" as a concept that demeans the executives, because it paints them as impatient people with short attention spans. But that criticism misses the boat, in my view. Coloring Books is about being respectful of your audience's time. It puts a premium on being crisp, clear, and concise.

Remember those three C's whenever you set about being the First Guy on Paper. Don't waste time down in the weeds. Keep it simple.

8.5 How the Irish Saved Civilization

A few years back, historian Thomas Cahill had a big success with a book titled, "How the Irish Saved Civilization." It told the story of how St. Patrick brought Christianity to Ireland in the 5th century and then helped transform the island into a place where literacy and learning were highly valued.

The fact that Ireland became "the isle of saints and scholars" is only the starting point for Cahill's story, however. About the time of St. Patrick, the continent of Europe was starting to be threatened by barbarians. Before long, the Roman Empire collapsed altogether.

Europe then plunged into the millennium-long Dark Ages. During that time, the European mainland lost pretty much all of its connections with the priceless knowledge and cultural wisdom that had been handed down from the Greeks, the Romans, and the Egyptians.

In Ireland, it was a different story. There, armed with the spirit of literacy St. Patrick had sparked and nourished, the monks kept voluminous records of all that priceless knowledge, keeping it safe for future generations.

Those Irish monks weren't technically the first guys on paper. In a sense, they were actually the *last* guys on paper. But as the Dark Ages went on, they turned out to be the *only* guys on paper, which is how they came to the rescue of Western Civilization.

8.6 The "Patterson Plan"

My brother Robert spent much of his career as a real estate developer. He worked for a major bank that was always adding new branches and locations around the country — and he ended up in charge of buying lots of land and buildings over the years.

These things tend to run in cycles, of course. Eventually, the bank got out of expansion mode and started to reverse gears and unload its properties. They told my brother to go into divestment mode.

My brother looked at the logistics of selling all these thousands of individual pieces of real estate in all these different towns and cities one by one, in a piecemeal manner. As you might imagine, that wasn't a pretty picture.

Instead, he devised a plan to sell all the real estate in one fell swoop — to a real estate investment trust. He found a prospect interested in such a deal and put down his plan for how to handle the transaction on paper.

He also went an extra step that perfectly fits with the spirit of Rule #8. On the title page of the plan, the first words he wrote were:

The Patterson Plan

Putting his name on the plan allowed him to maintain tighter control of the situation. He would be the person with the authority to decide which, if any, of the coming barrage of proposed changes and revisions would make it into the plan. After all, the plan had his name on it—it only made sense that everything in it needed his approval.

Robert was taking a risk, too, of course. If the plan didn't work, that failure would have his name on it. But sometimes in the process of getting things on paper, it makes perfect sense to put your name right up front and your reputation on the line.

8.7 The Bottom Line

Rule #1 situations are never smooth affairs. They tend, as a Bette Davis character might say, to be bumpy rides, full of vexing twists and surprising turns. There are two primary reasons why it is so important to take just a few extra minutes to document some of the most important of those twists and turns.

The first is that it will bring added clarity to your dealings with Rule #1 people. If their memory goes haywire at some point—and it probably will—there will be evidence on paper that their memory is, in fact, wrong. When they get into survival mode and deny having agreed to do something they failed to do, there will be evidence on paper that they are mistaken.

The second reason is that Rule #1 situations are often dicey affairs. They can end in failure. They can involve strained relationships and bruised egos. Most of the time it's the cool, level-headed character who has the record of what happened and who will emerge with his or her reputation intact. Make sure that person is you.

But, remember, we are not talking here about writing long diary entries about day-to-day minutiae in the workplace. We are talking about writing down a few bullet points about key moments—the birth of a project, the new strategic direction, and the like. Being The First Guy on Paper should never be a time-consuming affair.

Tangent—Say It Out Loud

Here's an addendum to the importance of putting everything down on paper. In the workplace, clarity is king. That applies to verbal communication as well as written.

I learned this the hard way as a young manager. I allowed too many meetings to break up without taking the time to make sure that everyone was on the same page when it came to our priorities and our action steps going forward.

Rule #1 characters flourish in such an atmosphere. Any murkiness when it comes to plans and next steps gives them the freedom to run off down whatever crazy sidetrack strikes their fancy.

Say It out Loud is the strategy that helped me to overcome this weakness. It comes into play at the end of meetings, during that period when the agenda items have been checked off and there's a feeling in the room that things are wrapping up.

Just when people are starting to gather their things together, I would jump in and say, "Stop. Nobody goes anywhere until we 'Say It Out Loud.'"

Once everyone settled back in, we would take a few extra moments to make sure there was consensus in the room about what the next steps would be and who was going to be responsible for taking them. This strategy is actually a good one to adopt as a general rule of workplace behavior, regardless of whether any Rule #1 people are in the room. Nor does the size of the group matter—Say It out Loud works just as well in meetings of two people as it does in meetings of 12.

Once you get in the habit of taking the time to Say It Out Loud, it will become that much easier to take the next step and put the priorities, action steps, and other items that everyone agreed to on paper.

BAG OF SHIT THEORY

Rule #9 - The Bag of Shit Theory

9.0 The Concept

Rule #1 situations can come in all sorts of shapes and sizes. They often involve encounters with illogical colleagues or impossible bosses. They can also arise when you need to navigate through a department or organization that has descended into bureaucratic craziness. And sometimes Rule #1 situations arrive seemingly out of the blue, such as when workplace stars align in such a way that it leaves you or your team facing a deadline so impossible that it is driving you crazy.

Rule #9 is a strategy designed to help manage the expectations people have as you make your way through a Rule #1 situation. The basic theory is this: If someone ends up in an assignment that is, well, a Bag of Shit, that person should make sure that everyone around the situation knows precisely what it is.

In fact, they should Say It Out Loud: "This is a Bag of Shit."

9.1 Pulling a Kevin

Credit for the Bag of Shit Theory goes to a former colleague of mine at the consulting firm. That company was a very large operation that played on a national stage with a high-powered clientele. We charged big-time prices. No one called us in to tackle the easy jobs.

Pretty much everything we took on was a Bag of Shit, to one degree or another.

Most young managers at the firm, including myself, took these jobs on without much fuss or complaint. No matter how tough the road ahead promised to be, we would nod our heads like good soldiers.

"Yes, sir, I can take care of this," we would say. "I'll get on it right away."

But one guy, Kevin, refused to play the good-soldier game. Every time he got a new assignment, a big scowl would come across his face. Then he'd start shaking his head in dismay.

"Whoa, wait a minute," he would say. "Do you have any idea how hard this is going to be?"

Kevin would then proceed to explain in great detail just what made the job a Bag of Shit and why the odds in his new assignment were stacked against success. He would always question whether he had enough resources to do the job right. And he would warn everyone that there were going to be lots of bumps in the road ahead.

He would keep up that sort of chatter all throughout the job as well. When giving progress reports, Kevin would never say that things were on track towards a successful outcome. Instead, no matter how smoothly things were going, he would tick off a lengthy list of problems that lay ahead.

"We're just starting to get into the critical stuff now," he would say in a typical report. "We should see pretty soon if we're going to be able to pull this miracle off without needing that extra time that I warned you about."

All of us young good-soldier managers used to laugh about this. We even had a name for it: "Pulling a Kevin."

But the more my career progressed, the more I came to see that there was a good amount of workplace wisdom in Kevin's approach. He may have overdone it at times, taking the Bag of Shit stuff to a level where it sometimes resembled a workplace version of The Boy Who Cried Wolf.

But eventually I came to see that Kevin was a better workplace strategist than I gave him credit for in my younger years. Most of the time Kevin wasn't lying or exaggerating when he called his assignment a Bag of Shit. He was just making sure that everyone involved knew that the task ahead was going to be difficult and that the outcome was likely to be something other than perfect.

When the inevitable bumps in the road appeared, Kevin didn't need to report it as a setback. Instead, he would report it as an "I-told-you-so" item. The same was true of the times he had to request extra time or resources to finish a job. Once Kevin had called Bag of Shit, there would be no shame or sense of failure attached to such requests.

And on those rare occasions when Kevin did manage to finish a Bag of Shit without encountering any serious setbacks, he was hailed as a hero who triumphed in the face of long odds. When we good-soldier types achieved that kind of outcome, we got no such acclaim. We had not prepared the ground as effectively as Kevin would have.

9.2 Playing the Expectations Game

In one sense, The Bag of Shit Theory is about managing the expectations of others. You want your supervisors and colleagues to recognize when you're up against some Rule #1 craziness. You want them to anticipate the bumpy ride ahead. You want them to be impressed if and when you actually achieve some measure of success with the Bag of Shit you've been handed.

But Rule #9 is also about managing your own expectations. People who are good at what they do grow accustomed over time to being successful. They come to expect themselves to hit a home run every time at bat.

But no one hits a home run every time. Sometimes you need to settle for a walk or a single. That's especially true in Rule #1 situations, when the odds of some less-than-perfect outcomes are much greater than normal.

Being clear-eyed and rational about this is important. It helps us to keep our cool when things start to go awry. It helps us to recognize when it's time to stop swinging for the fences and start looking for a way to just get on base.

9.3 The Call Center Miracle

Whenever I think about the Bag of Shit Theory, I remember a day at the insurance company when we received some dreadful news. A call center that was the hub of one of our side ventures was going out of business. The owners of the center were invoking a 60-day out clause in their contract.

This is a perfect example of how Rule #1 situations can materialize almost out of the blue, without anyone to blame. I do not know if that situation at that call center involved any Rule #1 characters. The company had always done a reasonably good job for us.

And then—*poof!*—they were gone. This created a mess of the first order for the insurance company. We were basically running an entire business operation through this one call center, and there was simply no way we could afford to put the operation in mothballs while we sorted things out.

A young woman named Janet stepped up in this moment of crisis. She pitched an emergency plan for managing the transition to a new center and getting it done on the impossibly short time frame. We signed off on her plan and wished her Godspeed.

Janet was a good-soldier type, just like I used to be in my younger days. She didn't say a word to anyone about just how big a Bag of Shit she had just volunteered to take care of. Instead, she simply went out and set about getting the job done.

I'm not sure how she pulled it off, but she did. Sixty days later, the entire operation was up and running in a new call center. I'm pretty certain Janet devoted just about every night and weekend of those two months to making it work. But she didn't tell anybody about that, either.

She made it look relatively easy. I think that was a mistake on her part, actually. Once the new call center was up and running, there were a few hiccups. Some of the customer service protocols in the new center weren't up to our usual standards. That sparked some griping from managers about Janet's performance on the call center assignment.

Janet took the criticism hard. She came to my office, looking for help in figuring out how best to respond.

"I don't understand where this is coming from," she said. "I thought I did a really great job in a really difficult assignment, and here it ends up with people badmouthing me."

I told Janet about the Bag of Shit Theory. All things considered, she did deserve better treatment from her colleagues, but in a way, she had brought it on herself.

If she had called Bag of Shit from the beginning, everyone involved might have seen in a clearer fashion just how challenging the call center crisis was. They might have expected to see bumps in the road. They might have been pleasantly surprised when those bumps turned out to be rather minor affairs that had no real impact on business results over the long term.

If she had called Bag of Shit, Janet could have put herself in position to respond to the griping with words like these: "I've been telling you from the beginning that this is an impossible timetable and that there are bound to be a few hiccups on customer service and in some other areas. Why are you acting like this is some surprise I'm springing on you?"

But alas, Janet had failed to call Bag of Shit. At the end of that visit to my office, she promised to put the theory to good use in the future.

9.4 Churchill on the Level

When Winston Churchill became prime minister on May 10, 1940, it was not exactly a promising time for Great Britain. That very day, the German army invaded Luxembourg, the Netherlands, and Belgium. The Battle of Belgium would be a short one, lasting all of 18 days. France would be the next domino to fall.

England was pretty much alone in the world. The United States would not join the conflict for another 18 months. The Russians had signed a non-aggression pact with the Germans. Many prominent Britons thought the time had come to accept reality and make a peace deal with Hitler.

Three days after taking office, Churchill stood before the Parliament to ask that they approve some new Cabinet appointments. He kept his remarks brief and to the point. His words were inspiring, but they also contained a brutally honest warning that a long run of very difficult days loomed ahead.

"We have before us an ordeal of the most grievous kind. We have before us many, many long months of struggle and of suffering. You ask, what is our policy? I can say: It is to wage war, by sea, land and air, with all our might and with all the strength that God can give us; to wage war against a monstrous tyranny, never surpassed in the dark, lamentable catalogue of human crime. That is our policy. You ask, what is our aim? I can answer in one word: It is victory, victory at all costs, victory in spite of all terror, victory, however long and hard the road may be; for without victory, there is no survival. Let that be realized; no survival for the British Empire, no survival for all that the British Empire has stood for, no survival for the urge and impulse of the ages, that mankind will move forward towards its goal. But I take up my task with buoyancy and hope. I feel sure that our cause will not be suffered to fail among men. At this time I feel entitled to claim the aid of all, and I say, come then, let us go forward together with our united strength."

What Churchill said that day was basically this: "England is holding a Bag of Shit, and I want to make sure my fellow citizens see that as clearly as I do."

9.5 Robert and Boomer under the Golden Dome

You can't always implement the Bag of Shit Strategy, but at least you understand what happened when things turn out in unexpected ways.

My brother Robert went to work for IBM right after earning his undergraduate degree from Notre Dame. He started out working sales in a territory managed by the company's Detroit office. He had a first-rate boss who went by the nickname of Boomer.

Robert and Boomer were on the scene for one of the seminal moments in the history of computing — the release of the IBM S/360 back in 1965. For obvious reasons, Boomer put Notre Dame on Robert's hit list of sales prospects.

Early on in that long sales campaign, Robert found himself standing next to Boomer under the famed Golden Dome on campus. They were on a balcony, two or three flights up when Boomer turned to Robert and said, "You know, don't you, that there's no freaking way in hell you're ever going to sell our computer to Notre Dame?"

Sometimes, there are great bosses like Boomer whose job nonetheless requires that they hand out Rule #1 assignments. Boomer sensed that Robert was young and inexperienced. He wanted to make sure that Robert understood that he was being handed a Bag of Shit—and that his boss would take that into account in judging his performance.

In the end, Robert turned that Bag of Shit into a pot of gold. Notre Dame eventually bought $15 million worth of IBM S/360s. Robert had the computers decked out in custom blue-and-gold panels.

Robert deserved to be treated like a conquering hero for this deal, but alas, that's not how things worked out. Shortly after that miracle sale, IBM shifted control of Robert's territory to the Chicago office.

Robert's new boss had no idea that the Notre Dame assignment was a Bag of Shit. He had no idea what a miracle Robert had pulled off. Much to Robert's chagrin, his quotas going forward were now based on Notre Dame-sized sales being the expected norm in his job performance.

Every once in a while, the Rule #1 rain is going to pour down on you, and there will be not much you can do about it. It's like an old blues song, "If it wasn't for Rule #1 luck, I wouldn't have no luck at all." I hope that little lyric helps you keep things in perspective if and when you get drenched like Robert did after that Notre Dame miracle.

9.6 Stoplight Communications

"We need to talk."

Those can be ominous words in just about any circumstances. But when spoken by a Rule #1 character who then proceeds to close the door to your office, they can be especially alarming. One strategy we managers devised at one company where I used to work is to quickly interrupt the bearers of seemingly bad news.

"Stop right there," we would say. "Is it red, yellow, or green?"

What we wanted to hear, of course, was an evaluation of how serious a problem we had on our hands. If a problem was red, that meant we would need to stop what we're doing right this instant and pay attention to this new problem. Yellow and green would be lesser affairs.

As we've seen, many Rule #1 people suffer from illogical thinking patterns. They often struggle to keep their emotions in check, and they have a tendency to overreact in the face of roadblocks or setbacks.

The Stoplight Strategy is an attempt to force them into a more normal way of processing a new development. It's a tool that can help make sure a Rule #1 person takes the time to pause and evaluate the seriousness of the problem before they launch into a panicky report.

It's a strategy that can prevent some of the unnecessary workplace drama that so often arises in Rule #1 situations.

9.7 The Bottom Line

For the most part, people tend to take on assignments in their work life with the approach of a good soldier. Even when the assignment is a crazy one, full of potential roadblocks and complications, we nod our heads, say, "Yes, ma'am," and get started on the task.

In Rule #1 situations, that is not a wise choice. The road ahead is bound to be rocky. A successful outcome is going to be quite difficult to achieve—perhaps even out of reach.

That's where Rule #9 comes in. It adjusts everyone's expectations right at the outset so that they are in line with what is actually likely to happen. In an assignment where the chances of success seem dicey, it's important to make that clear from the outset.

When you get handed a Bag of Shit, be sure to speak up and let everyone know exactly what it is that you're holding.

Tangent—The Pottery Barn Rule

Back in 2002, as the United States considered going to war in Iraq, U.S. Secretary of State Colin Powell issued a famous warning to President George W. Bush.

"You are going to be the proud owner of 25 million people," he told the president. "You will own all their hopes, aspirations, and problems. You'll own it all."

This eventually came to be known as the "Pottery Barn rule," used in the sense of: "You break it, you own it." It always sounded to my ears like Powell was "pulling a Kevin" and pointing out that there was a potential Bag of Shit on the horizon.

Rule #10 - It's Never Too Late to Do It Right

10.0 The Concept

Most people strive every day to put in their best effort and tackle their jobs with integrity and honesty. A stretch of Rule #1 rain can make sticking to those principles more of a challenge. Crazy situations take crazy turns. Projects get sidetracked and delayed. Tasks get left undone. Mistakes are made.

Faced with such difficulties, there will be those who want to take shortcuts and settle for something less than success.

Resist that temptation. Effort, integrity, and honesty are just as important in Rule #1 rainstorms as they are in the rest of your life. Here in Rule #10, we look at coping strategies for Rule #1 situations that will help make sure that you can hold your head up high by striving for the best possible outcome in a difficult situation.

How many times have we heard "we don't have time to do it right". The usual outcome is a botched deliverable or so much time spent doing it wrong that it would have been quicker to stop and do it right anyway.

10.1 Do the Right Thing

In order to Do It Right, we need to do the right thing. This, too, is not going to be easy.

Rarely in Rule #1 situations will the right course of action be clear. There are no so-called "Pearl Harbor Scenarios," in which the next necessary step of declaring war on Japan is blindingly obvious to one and all, when the Rule #1 rain is falling.

Be aware that you will probably hear a lot of naysaying. There is not enough time for this, not enough money for that, and not enough expertise for some other thing.

While issued with great sincerity, these warnings will often be mistaken. The Fixer always understood this. The day he would arrive on a project, the first order he would issue was for everyone to stop working altogether. Every time he did this, The Fixer heard howls about how there wasn't enough time for a stoppage, and every time he ignored them.

Lots of people, and especially Rule #1 people, get all caught up in deadlines and budgets that can often turn out to be more artificial than real. What if spending 10 percent over the budget got you to an outcome that is 100 percent better? What would the company rather have—a bad project that arrives on time, or an acceptable one that arrives a few weeks or months late?

This book is more about processes and strategies than it is about morals and ethics. But in the end, striving to see the big picture clearly and do the right thing is going to be a piece of the puzzle that protects you from losing your way in the Rule #1 rain.

10.2 "Gentlemen, this is a football"

The fact that his name is on the trophy that they give to the team that wins the Super Bowl should give you an idea about just how successful a football coach Vince Lombardi was. His Green Bay Packers won the first two Super Bowls, in 1967 and 1968.

When Lombardi arrived in Green Bay in 1959, the team was in disarray. The year before, the Packers had endured their worst season ever, winning just one game. Fans weren't coming out to the games. The league was worried whether the franchise would survive.

Lombardi soon established himself as the type of coach who demanded maximum dedication and focus. He was obsessive about paying attention to the fundamentals of the game.

At one point during his first training camp, Lombardi grew frustrated with the lack of effort his players were bringing to practice. He blew the whistle and told everyone to gather around him.

Then he picked up a ball and launched into a famous speech that began with these words: "Gentlemen, this is a football." Lombardi then proceeded to tell his players about yard markers, goal posts, end zones, and all the other basics of the game that every one of his players had known about by the age of six.

His message? The Green Bay Packers are going to play the game the right way. They will be a team that pays heed to the fundamentals. And they will be a team that prepares for the coming season by focusing first and foremost on those fundamentals.

As the years went on, the "Gentlemen, this is a football" speech became a Packer tradition. Lombardi would deliver it every year at the beginning of training camp, reinforcing for his players each time his vision for the team and his expectations of his players. Over the years the speech became a sort of promise—that if his players would learn to play the game the right way, they would find success.

Lombardi's Packers turned things around quickly. They went 7-4 in 1959. Lombardi was named the league's Coach of the Year. And Packers fans returned in droves, selling out every game of the 1960 season. In fact, the Packers have had a full house for every game after that, right up through to today.

10.3 The "Risk of Finishing" Test

Once Rule #1 comes into play on a project, the odds are that it will run into serious trouble and perhaps fail to achieve its full goals. One thing to remember upon realizing that a Rule #1 situation is at hand is take a step back and take a clear-eyed look at the stakes involved in the situation.

The world is constantly on the move while we are working our way towards the finish lines on the various tasks and projects in our lives. Time passes. Circumstances change. Technology advances. People come and go. Priorities shift.

Ask yourself a few questions: What would happen if we walked away from this project, just left it undone? Have things in the company changed since this project got under way, making it less important than it used to be?

Perhaps when the job was launched six months before, it was the boss's pet project, the one she watched over like a hawk. But two months ago she got promoted out of the department. Does the new boss care about the project? Would he even notice if it just went away?

My friend Betty has a good story along these lines. She used to run a small nonprofit group in the town where she lives. She started in that job just when the economy went south back in 2008. One of the state grants she inherited from her predecessor offered a bit of help to property owners who took on major projects to fix up commercial buildings.

After the real estate market tanked, however, no one was starting any big repair jobs. Betty went along quarter after quarter, filling in her reports to the state and telling them that no one was accessing their grant money. She put out press releases, made phone calls, and knocked on doors, trying to sell a product no one wanted.

Eventually, she decided to level with her grant manager. Nervously, she told the woman that she saw no hope on the horizon that these grant dollars would get used anytime soon in her town. She told the woman that maybe those dollars would be better spent elsewhere, rather than sitting around doing nothing.

Betty had some bad experiences with Rule #1 bureaucrats over the years, but this wasn't one of them. The grant manager's response took her by surprise.

The manager said that Betty's organization could give back the remaining grant money with no harm whatsoever to its reputation and its future grant projects. In fact, such a give back would be a very positive mark going forward with state grant reviewers—an indication that Betty's group was an organization that could be trusted to do the right thing.

Once she did a little digging and performed The Risk of Finishing Test, Betty found that there was no risk at all. She soon set that project aside and got onto other, more productive things. As Rule #1 situations arise, step back and take a hard look at how important a project is. Maybe it doesn't need doing at all.

10.4 Hail Mary Plays

Let's return to football for another moment. One play that helps make the game so popular is the dramatic "Hail Mary Pass." That's when the quarterback of the team that's losing throws a last-ditch long bomb just as the clock is ticking down to zero.

When a team connects on such a play, their fans tend to remember and cherish the moment for a lifetime. They do this precisely because the touchdowns scored by way of the Hail Mary are out-and-out miracles. The odds are so stacked against the losing team by that point in the game that the only option left was to throw the ball as far as your quarterback can and hope that something incredibly lucky happens.

People in the business world try Hail Mary plays, too. They can seem like a tempting option—a way to solve all of your business problems in one fell swoop. Quite a few businesses fell victim to that temptation on the night of Super Bowl XXXIV in January 2000.

Known in marketing lore as the "Dotcom Super Bowl," it featured television ads from no fewer than 14 dotcom companies. Combined, they spent $44 million on the ads. One of the biggest buyers was a small Florida-based company called Our Beginning. They were in the business of wedding invitations.

The owner was sure that a Super Bowl ad would "put a turbo charge in the company" by getting its name in front of "the largest captive audience of the year." He spent $5 million on the plan, including $1 million on website upgrades so that it could handle a slew of new traffic.

In the first quarter of 2000, Our Beginning did half a million dollars in sales. One researcher calculated that they spent $2,800 to acquire each new individual customer, and that customer then spent $280 with them.

That is about how Hail Mary passes usually turn out in the business world. The site ourbeginning.com is now home to a Seattle-based daycare facility.

Miracles do in fact happen sometimes, but betting your whole project one coming along just when you need it is never a recommended strategy in Rule #1 situations.

Hail Mary's usually end up being Fail Mary's.

10.5 Release the Pressure, Then Decide

Deadlines are generally good things. They motivate us to get projects done in a timely way and on a schedule that's good for the bottom line.

But in Rule #1 situations, deadlines can also become a source of "FUD." Do you remember FUD from Rule #3? It's an acronym for all of the "fear, uncertainty, and doubt" that impossible people like to throw around in order to deflect attention from themselves.

Projects where Rule #1 comes into play often go badly awry. When that happens, the original deadlines assigned to a project at the starting gate become more and more difficult to reach. Such deadlines can generate an enormous amount of pressure on a project.

It's important to be on the lookout for times when that deadline pressure is simply too intense and there is an atmosphere of panic in the air. Is it getting in the way of your ability to think straight and perform like a professional?

In such situations, deadlines are just like rules—they are made to be broken. Release the deadline pressure, then start making decisions about next steps with a mindset that is calm and rational.

10.6 The Perils of Perfectionism

On the other hand… Harry Truman is reported to have said he wanted to hire only one armed economists so they could not say "On the other hand". So, on the other hand, there is often a balance to be found to achieve real success.

We met The Fixer back in Rule #3. He was the guy my old consulting firm called in when a big job was falling apart at the seams. The Fixer had a quality that I came to think of as a "focus on the finish."

By the time he arrived on the scene, everything involved in the project had fallen apart. Scores upon scores of people were flailing about in desperation. No one was making any real progress. And all of these people had come into the project at the outset with visions of perfect, award-winning endings dancing in their heads.

Have you heard the old saying "The perfect is the enemy of the good". It's generally attributed to Voltaire. And what it means is that oftentimes striving for perfection ends up being a big waste of time. You expend enormous energy and get miniscule improvements. You should have stopped and moved on once you got to something acceptable and functional.

There is another clever saying that gets at this phenomenon. Robert Watson-Watt, who invented early warning radar, once said, "Give them the third best to go on with; the second best comes too late, the best never comes."

The Fixer never allowed himself to fall into the trap of thinking that the only acceptable outcome was a perfect one. The way he looked at success, it could come in a variety of different shapes and sizes. And it could come on a variety of different timelines as well.

He taught me to keep an open mind about outcomes. He always seemed to be studying the path ahead, looking for the route that would lead to the biggest measure of success that was still achievable for a reasonable amount of effort and expense.

It's almost like he had a reset button. That button would allow The Fixer to constantly refresh his vision of a project and adjust his goals for it in response to changing circumstances and new information. That flexible focus on the finish was a big part of The Fixer's success in bringing failing projects back from the brink.

10.7 The Bottom Line

Coping with Rule #1 situations is always difficult. With crazy people doing crazy things, how could it be otherwise?

Suddenly, short cuts can seem quite tempting. This will be especially true when a deadline is approaching. That's when everyone around you will start making the case that there is simply not enough time to do the job right.

Walking away from such Rule #1 situations will also be a temptation, but that usually is not a viable option. The obligations of life—to our companies, co-workers, patients, students, etc.—generally require us to soldier on through the Rule #1 rain.

The best course of action is to put on some metaphorical rain gear and get about the business of doing It Right— that's the right thing to do. The final outcome ahead may not match all of the rosy pictures of success that were painted at the outset, but it still needs to be the best outcome achievable under difficult circumstances. Be The Fixer.

Tangent—The Gordian Knot

Have you ever heard of this legend from ancient Greece? The story goes like this: The province of Phrygia had a great king named Gordias, and before he died he tied up an ox-cart with a knot so intricate that no one over the course of many centuries was able to undo it.

Hundreds upon hundreds of men had tried and failed by the time Alexander the Great rolled into town. But even he struggled at first to find the end of the rope that would allow him to untangle the whole knot. Instead of keeping at it pointlessly, however, Alexander stopped, reoriented himself, and took a completely fresh look at the problem.

Then he pulled out his sword and sliced the knot in half.

Throughout this book, that's the kind of creativity and resourcefulness I've been encouraging you to embrace. In dealing with impossible people, it's high time we all started thinking like Alexander. Keep your cool. Take a fresh look. Adopt a new attitude.

Epilogue – So, What Have You Learned, Dorothy?

11.0 The Concept

It's time, once again, to Say It Out Loud, the strategy from Rule #8. It comes into play at the end of meetings, right at that moment when people start gathering up their papers and reaching for their bags. We've reached that point in this book. It's time to stop and make sure that everyone is in a confident place, ready to put our strategies into action the next time they run into some Rule #1 rain.

11.1 The Rules in Review

Mark this page. It's where you can come back to if and when Rule #1 arises again in your life and you find yourself in need of a quick review. We also have handy wallet cards available—just go to www.Rule-Num-One.com if you don't have one already.

Rule #1—Crazy People Make You Crazy: Rule #1 people live on the unmoored side of life's seesaw. Up there, they are detached from many of the basic rules of human interaction—things like common sense, logical thinking, reciprocity, and fair play. They are living by different rules.

What that means is that crazy people will do crazy things. And it's not just people who do crazy things. Companies can operate in crazy Rule #1 ways. So can government agencies, hospitals, and universities. It's easy for those of us living on the grounded side of life's seesaw to get sucked into that craziness. Rule #1 people and institutions can be contagious. Their behavior can drive you to the point of tearing your hair out, throwing tantrums, and making rash, ill-advised decisions.

In short, crazy people make you crazy.

Rule #2—Am *I* Crazy? Here on the grounded side of life's seesaw, the basic rules of human interaction include giving other people the benefit of the doubt. This is a good, admirable habit, but sometimes it makes it more difficult to recognize Rule #1 behavior for what it is.

Instead, we start wondering what it is that we ourselves are doing wrong. "Am I crazy?" That is the question that should stop you dead in your tracks. When you start to question your own sanity, there probably is some Rule #1 craziness going on. But it's time to stop looking in the mirror and start looking around, because asking that question means you are not the one who is crazy.

Rule #3 — FUD: Rule #1 people generally like to keep their craziness under wraps. When they sense that their secret is in danger of being exposed, they tend to go into a panicky mode in which they try to draw attention away from themselves.

This tendency operates very much like the "fight-or-flight" instinct, except that in the Rule #1 world there is a third option — "FUD." It's an acronym for fear, uncertainty, and doubt. It comes into play when Rule #1 people raise scary new issues and potential problems in order to distract you from the issues that really need your attention.

It's important to recognize this misdirection play when it arises. Not only will deciphering FUD help you identify a Rule #1 character, it will also keep you focused on the issues where you can make a genuine difference.

Rule #4 — Count the Bricks: Rule #1 people live in a day-to-day world, disconnected from any sort of long-term considerations about results and consequences. This is why they so often deliver sunny progress reports when they haven't made much progress at all. They simply want to get through the current moment. They are not even thinking about the risk of getting found out weeks or months down the line.

If you're worried that Rule #1 is in play, Rule #4 can help you make the call. Count the Bricks is a strategy that involves setting up clear, objective measures of progress —

measures that guarantee you will see tangible, physical evidence of progress, rather than relying on verbal reassurances.

Rule #5 — Think Twice About First Impressions: First impressions are mysterious things. On the one hand, we are told that they are usually right, and on the other hand, we are told that you can't judge a book by its cover. Deciding once and for all whether Rule #1 is at hand can be quite a challenge, especially since the decision often ends up being based on such impressions.

In Rule #5, we shared a number of decision-making strategies that will help you to step back and re-evaluate your first impressions. That will put you in position to make calm, logical calls about whether a situation really is a Rule #1 affair and how serious of a problem it presents.

Rule #6 — Trouble Now Is Trouble Later: With Rule #6, we moved from strategies that help you identify Rule #1 situations to ones that help you cope with the craziness. Dealing with Rule #1 people is hard. It often involves having difficult conversations and dealing with raw emotions.

But it is a task that must be tackled. What Rule #6 says is that if left untended Rule #1 trouble is bound to get worse and worse going forward. Carpe diem. The day that you realize Rule #1 is in effect is the day to start taking calm, smart, and disciplined action to protect yourself from the Rule #1 rain.

Rule #7—If It Feels Good, Don't Say It: Rule #7 is all about staying in control and maintaining a calm, rational mindset. This, too, can be quite difficult in Rule #1 situations, since crazy people behave in ways that can be extremely frustrating.

No matter how good it would feel to tell off a Rule #1 person, you must never show your anger to him or her. Your anger serves to give them more Rule #1 ammunition, allowing them to feel like a victim and put you in the role of irrational aggressor. Keep your anger in check at all times.

Rule #8—First Guy on Paper Wins: Winston Churchill once said, "History will be kind to me for I intend to write it." Those are words you should heed as Rule #1 situations unfold. Because they are living on the unmoored side of life's seesaw, irrational people often have a loose grasp on day-to-day realities. They can recall events that never happened, and they can recount conversations that never occurred.

Take the initiative by spending just a few extra moments building a simple paper trail. After a meeting, write a quick email that confirms what action steps were agreed to. Jot down brief-as-can-be notes in your calendar about who agreed to do what. This will put you in a stronger position down the road. You will be the one with a clear record of what happened when in the event that things get off track.

Rule #9—The Bag of Shit Theory: Too many of us tend to operate in good-soldier mode, taking even the most difficult assignments on with a simple, "Yes, ma'am, I can do that, and I'll get on it right away." This is not a wise approach in Rule #1 situations, which are so often fraught with difficulty and at risk for unsuccessful or imperfect outcomes.

What we should do instead when someone hands us a Bag of Shit is make sure that the relevant people understand that it is, indeed, a Bag of Shit. That way, no one will be surprised when difficulties and troubles arise. And because everyone saw at the outset that such troubles were likely to arise, the troubles won't come off as the result of your own personal failures.

Rule #10—It's Never Too Late To Do It Right: Most of us tackle our work every day with a commitment to integrity and honesty. Sticking to those commitments can be difficult in Rule #1 situations, especially as the bad news piles up—mistakes are made, tasks are left undone, and deadlines are missed.

Suddenly, short cuts can seem quite tempting. This will be especially true when a deadline is approaching. That's when everyone around you will start making the case that there is simply not enough time to do the job right.

Rule #10 says that there are few situations where finishing a job in the wrong way will result in a good outcome.

More likely, the short-cut approach will end in the slow, painful unwinding of a failed project.

11.2 The Mind Is What Matters

Back in Chapter 1, I told you that this short, simple anecdote would be the most important one in the whole book:

My sister went on a vacation to Ireland a few years back. When I asked her how she enjoyed the trip, she jumped straight into gushing with boundless joy.

"Wonderful!" she said. "It was such a beautiful, enchanting place filled with these incredibly warm and happy and generous people. Standing on the Cliffs of Moher, that was just one of the great experiences of my life—something I'll never forget."

I asked her about the weather.

"Oh, it rained every day," *she said with a laugh and a dismissive wave of her hand.*

If there's one thing that I hope you've learned in this book, it's that the most important steps you can take in dealing with impossible people involve adjusting your own attitude and expectations. Action-step items can be helpful, but they are secondary by comparison to the work that happens inside your mind.

Into every life a little Rule #1 rain must fall. That is a simple fact of life, and facing up to it is step one on your journey to a place in life where you stop allowing impossible people to suck up too much of your time and emotional energy.

Once you accept the fact that Rule #1 rain is inevitable, there will be no reason to pull your hair out in frustration when an impossible person appears in your life.

It's also important to understand both that Rule #1 situations will keep happening and that they are never easy to deal with. Set your expectations accordingly. Back in my days with the consulting firm, a young guy who had come aboard recently asked me a sensible-sounding question. "Why is it that we keep getting all these incredibly hard jobs?"

But actually, the question did not make sense at all. I told him to think about the fact that we were a top-of-the-line firm that charged a whole lot of money for our services. Why would anyone call us in on the easy jobs?

"It's like being a fireman," I told him "Once you put that uniform on, you pretty much know that you're going to get fire calls."

The Rule #1 phenomenon is like that too. By simple virtue of the facts that we are social beings and that we work for a living, we are bound to run into Rule #1 characters and situations as we make our way through life. It really is as inevitable as the rain in Ireland and fire calls at the firehouse.

It's also important that we learn to treat that Rule #1 rain like my sister treated the rain in Ireland—as an annoyance rather than a disaster. Pick up your umbrella, choose the right clothing, and get about your day. In this case, of course, the rain gear takes the form of Rules #2 through 10, all of our tips for recognizing and dealing with impossible people. Life is too short to let Rule #1 people take control of your days. One more time:

Life is too short and too precious to allow ourselves to be side tracked by impossible people and the impossible problems they create.

The last thought: Remember your priorities in life. Getting through Rule #1 situations is about survival, not victory. It's about protecting your time and emotional energy so that you can spend them on the precious things in life rather than wasting them on a Rule #1 person who can't be fixed, no matter how many hours and how much energy you put into the project. Always keep your eyes on the real prizes of life, that combination of family and friends and hobbies and faith and community that gives you a sense of joy and fulfillment.

Thank you.

The Team

John J. Patterson – Author

Over a 38-year business career, Mr. Patterson held senior executive and consulting positions in a number of industries. Most positions were leadership roles in the Operations and Technology areas. He was EVP/COO for two companies, partner with a major global consulting firm, Co-founder, and president of a regional consulting company. In his early career, he was a production scheduler in a glass bottle factory, stereo salesman and later a computer programmer and project manager.

Mr. Patterson resides on Spring Branch Farm in Butler, Maryland with Katharine, his wife of almost 35 years. They have two wonderful daughters, Grace and Hannah. He and Katharine travel frequently, usually on birding tours.

Jim Duffy - Editor

Jim Duffy is a writer and entrepreneur based in Cambridge, MD. He has been an award-winning editor and writer at several regional magazines, including *Baltimore* and *Chesapeake Bay*. He holds an MA from Northwestern University. He has launched Secrets of the Eastern Shore, a business that develops products and books that help people celebrate and explore the Delmarva Peninsula.

Mark Hill – Illustrator

Mark Hill is a Boulder, Colorado-based cartoonist & illustrator and he began drawing when he was old enough to hold a crayon without also eating it. His work has been published in Time, Forbes and the Wall Street Journal, and he has illustrated over 30 books, (ranging from children's to business books.) His corporate clients include Bayer, Boeing, Cisco Systems, GM, Google, Intel Corp., Merck, Northwestern Mutual, Pepsi & Time Warner.